THE
MOORFIELD PIT
DISASTER

by

Harry Tootle

Landy Publishing
1998

© Copyright in the text of this book is held by Harry Tootle
ISBN 1 872895 38 7
British Library Cataloguing in Publication Data.
A catalogue record for this book is available from the British Library

This book is one of a limited edition of 1000.

Landy Publishing have also published:

A Lancashire Look: A Lancashire Book by Benita Moore
Lancashire, This, That an' t'other by Doris Snape
An Accrington Mixture edited by Bob Dobson
Accrington Observed by Bob Dobson and Brian Brindle
Accrington's Changing Face by Frank Watson and Bob Dobson
Threads of Lancashire Life by Winnie Bridges
The Really Lancashire Book edited by Bob Dobson

A full list of titles can be had from:

Landy Publishing
'Acorns'
3 Staining Rise
Staining
Blackpool
FY3 0BU
Tel/Fax 01253 895678

Design by Mike Clarke
Tel/Fax 01254 395848
Printed by Nayler the Printer, Church
Tel 01254 234247

Introduction

This work is dedicated to the men, women and children who toiled in the bowels of the earth. Many thousands of them lost their lives in the struggle to win the coal, which was commonly called 'Black Diamonds', and which eventually brought and sustained this nation at the forefront of the industrial world for over two hundred years.

One of the many who spent their working lives underground was Henry Doswell. He was born eighteen years after the Moorfield disaster on the 7th November 1901. He began working underground at Moorfield on his fifteenth birthday. For the next thirty years he worked at Moorfield, Whinney Hill and Martholme Collieries. He attended Burnley Municipal College to study mining technique. After five years at college he was appointed as Ventilation Officer at Moorfield. For most of his life he fought to have a lasting memorial to the memory of the men and boys who lost their lives in the Moorfield disaster of 1883. Henry Doswell died in October 1992 aged 90. I hope this book goes some way to fulfilling his wishes.

When reading this book the reader may find it difficult to understand some of the mining terminology. Throughout the book you will find certain words and phrases enclosed within single quotation marks. This is to signify that the subject can be found in the glossary at the end of the book. To assist anyone attempting to trace their family tree I have included all the information I have been able to find on the families of all those involved with the disaster at Moorfield.

I would like to thank all of those good people who gave so much of their time in helping me put this book together. They are Alan Davis of the Lancashire Museum of Mining; Jack Nadin; Ian Winstanley; John Davis; Big Dave Hodgson; Jack Broderick and especially Little June Huntingdon, whose research found for me so much obscure information, and whose red pen along with that of Susan Halstead's gave me a good lesson in basic English and saved me many hours of work. I must also thank the ladies of the Local Studies Library, Accrington. Without them where could one begin to research our local history? I have also to thank my lady wife Jacqueline, for her patience and understanding that I would eventually finish the book.

In the book I have tried to explain to the person with no knowledge of coal mining the technicalities of working in a Victorian pit and the dangers presented by methane gas when it mixed with poor quality air and a flame, and what after-effects the resulting explosion had.

I have also listed for the first time in over a century, along with the names of the dead and injured, some personal and family details. Be prepared - there is a great deal of sadness in these pages, for many lives were altered forever on the 7th November 1883.

Harry Tootle
August 1998

3

Moorfield Colliery around the turn of the century.

4

THE MOORFIELD COLLIERY EXPLOSION
7ᵀᴴ NOVEMBER 1883.

*"A man who has no interest in the past,
has no interest in the future,
And lives for the day alone."*

The first recorded instances of coal being mined in Clayton-le-Moors and Altham was in 1641. John Grimshaw let the coal seam at Clayton to Henry Towneley and Nicholas Towneley, of Royle for 18 years. In 1652 the coal getters or hewers were paid 4½d. per quarter; the drawers 3d; the banksman and his partner received 3½d. per quarter for winding and finding '*sleddes, shovels, and other things*'. There remained 4d. per quarter profit for the owner.

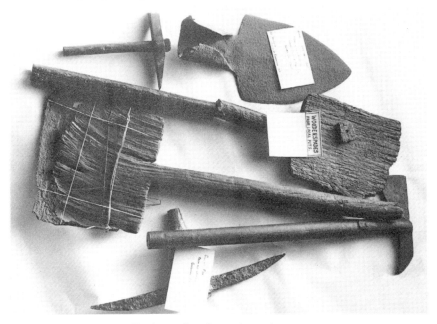

Tools used in the early coalmines.

Photo. John Davis

Between 1880 and 1890, there were no less than 22 major pit disasters in Britain, resulting in the deaths of 1,741 men and boys, many of them as young as ten years old. Many of the boys who died in the Moorfield Pit explosion were under the present school leaving age and today some of them would still be attending their junior school. In the case of John Thomas Hall, aged 15, he was his mother's sole means of support.

The 19th century attitude to life and death in the mining fraternity is hard for the modern mind to grasp. It would be wrong to suggest that life was cheap; the men went into the mines knowing the dangers to which they were exposing themselves. The owners chased their profits, resisting change and modernisation and the men had their wages to earn, working in conditions that put their life on the line every time they entered the pit. Both men and masters cut corners when it came to safety.

Sleddes were used to haul wicker baskets of coal to the shaft. Sleddes, also known as sledges, of a later date had wheels and ran on tracks.

Photo. John Davis

MOORFIELD COLLIERY

The Colliery and its Ventilation.

The colliery at Altham was originally named Altham Colliery and it is not known when it was renamed Moorfield. It was situated to the right-hand side of the A678 Blackburn to Burnley road, going towards Padiham, half a mile from the present traffic lights at the Hare and Hounds Hotel, Clayton-le-Moors. The entrance to the pit-yard was by the side of Pilkington's Bridge, which carried the main road over the Leeds and Liverpool canal. Pilkington's Bridge was known locally as 'Dickie Brig'. Moorfield Colliery has always been referred to as 'Dickie Brig Pit'. Very little remains of the original pithead buildings, most of the buildings still standing date from the years after the disaster in 1883.

The sinking of the Moorfield Pit began July 1879 and was completed in July 1881. The shaft was within 20 yds (18.3m) of the Leeds and Liverpool Canal. Water from the canal began to pour into the shaft during the sinking and to hold it back the shaft was lined with a cast iron 'tubbing'. It was then continued down 678 feet, (207m) to the 36- inch thick (1m) Upper Mountain seam.

Originally the mine would be worked as a single shaft pit, the shaft being divided down the centre by a 'brattice' (a wooden partition with the seams between the planks sealed with pitch). Air would travel down one side of the brattice, circulate round the workings, and return up the other side. There were several ways of creating a circulation of air. By using a furnace at the base of the upcast side of the shaft to create a draught of air, by using natural ventilation, or by windmill. It is not clear which one was in use at Moorfield at this time.

In 1862, at the Hartley Colliery, near Newcastle-upon-Tyne, the cast iron beam of the pumping engine broke away and fell into the shaft, taking the brattice and cage with it. The shaft was completely sealed, thereby entombing 204 men and boys. In 1864, a law was passed outlawing single shaft mines. As with many Acts of Parliament, the owners found ways to avoid complying with them. Numerous single shaft mines were still working years after the Act was passed. Many of the owners claimed they could not justify the cost of sinking a second shaft, and that they would have to work the mine until it could be linked-up with the workings of another colliery. This could have been the situation at Moorfield.

The colliery was owned by W. E. Taylor of the newly formed Altham Colliery Co. In 1868, the company was taken over by a partnership between James Barlow, the second Mayor of Accrington and J. J. Rippon, who also had an interest in the Great Harwood Colliery Co. The company also owned the Martholme and Whinney Hill collieries. James Barlow bought out Rippon's interest in the company in 1868. He extended his mining interests further when he bought out the Rippon family's interests in the Great Harwood Colliery Co. in 1892.

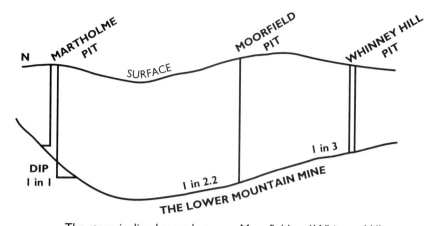

The steep inclined seam between Moorfield and Whinney Hill

Sectional plan of a coalmine using furnace ventilation.

It was around 1868 that the shaft at Moorfield was taken down a further 173 feet (53m) to the 28inch (711mm) thick Lower Mountain seam. Two stone drifts, 8ft. (2.45m) wide and 7ft (2.13m) high, were driven 1,200 yards (1,100m) from the base of the shaft to the shaft at Whinney Hill. One of the drifts, known as 'Billy Brow', became the engine plane, or main haulage road, along which ran an endless chain haulage system. It was powered by a twin-cylinder steam engine situated at the base of the Whinney Hill shaft. The steam for the engine was provided by the boilers on the surface and piped down the shaft.

The other drift, the return airway for both collieries, was the travelling road for the men. The roadway had 264 steps cut into the floor to help the men to climb the 1 in 6 incline. Originally there was a metal handrail down the centre of the road, to separate the men coming on shift from those going off. This enabled the men to pass each other without getting in each other's way.

One of the shafts at Whinney Hill then became the upcast shaft for both collieries. A furnace at the base of the shaft provided the draw for the ventilation, which worked on the 'split ventilation system'. The second shaft at Whinney Hill acted as a downcast for one section of the mine workings, the Moorfield shaft being the downcast for the other.

The shaft at Moorfield had the brattice removed and was fitted out with two double-decked cages. Each deck could carry four, 21 inch (914mm) high tubs, each with a capacity of $4^1/_2$ cwt. (228.6kg), or when 'man-riding' (i.e. carrying sixteen men, eight to a deck.)

Each ventilation system was separated by a series of doors, operated by the 'door tenters', to prevent the air being diverted from its course or the foul air mixing with the clean. The door tenters were the youngest of the boys employed in the pit. They would sit by the air door, and when they heard a 'drawer' coming along with a tub, they would open the door to let him through and close it again behind him. Should a drawer 'get himself without light', by accidentally extinguishing his lamp, he would take the lamp from the door tenter and leave the younger boy to sit hour upon hour in total darkness. For a ten-year-old this must have been a terrifying experience.

James Barlow sent for his son-in-law, George Watson Macalpine, at the time working as a marine engineer in Paisley, Scotland. He asked Macalpine to run the colliery company for him. Macalpine consented on the condition that he could buy the company out of his salary to which James Barlow agreed. Sir George made his final payment on the 5th July 1897 when James Barlow was on his deathbed. The Macalpine family were to retain their interest in the mines until nationalisation in 1947.

The Cause: Methane at Moorfield.

On the morning of the 7th November 1883, when the first of the men descended the shaft at Moorfield Colliery, they were entering an atmosphere which was primed like a bomb waiting to explode. All the elements were there, ready and waiting. In one of the headings off the N°. 2 level, gas was issuing from a 'rig', or fault, which

George Macalpine the owner of the collieries.
Mrs. Macalpine who with her servants attended the injured at Whinney Hill.

cut across the coalface. Four hours later this gas would be ignited to create a flash, which would set off the main explosive element, the coal dust. The coal dust had accumulated over the years, coating the walls, roof and timbers from the working places to the shaft. The men carried the Davy Safety Lamp into the pit with them. This was the fuse which was to set in motion the terrible force of the explosion; it would claim the lives of 68 men and boys.

Contrary to general belief, Sir Humphrey Davy was not the first man to invent the flame safety lamp. There had been several attempts to create a lamp which had the two essential ingredients; sufficient light when travelling and working and a barrier between the flame and the atmosphere. Many lamps had been invented, both in Britain and abroad, with a certain amount of success. Dr. William Reid Clanny invented the first practical lamp in 1813, for which he was awarded the Silver Medal by the Royal Society of Arts in 1816. His second improved lamp of 1817 gained him the Gold Medal from the Society. Both the lamps were large and needed an additional man to work them while the collier hewed the coal.

George Stevenson, a self-educated colliery engineer, tested his first lamp, the Tube and Slide lamp, at Killingworth Colliery, County Durham in 1815. For his work on the lamp, Stevenson was awarded £1000, raised by public donation, and the colliers gave him a silver watch.

Also in 1815, Sir Humphrey Davy scientifically investigated the properties of 'methane', a gas which results from the decay of organic matter. It is an odourless, colourless, hydrocarbon gas, which forms an explosive mixture when combined with air.

Although non-poisonous in itself, if a man was caught out by a sudden inrush of gas and was unable to get out of the workings fast enough, he would soon be overcome and suffocate. In earlier times a miner's first warning of the presence of gas was when he lost his light, as the gas snuffed out his candle. The gas was known to the miners as 'firedamp'. With a mixture of between 5% and 15% methane in the atmosphere, the flame in the safety lamp would begin to rise and flare. This in turn would heat up the wire gauze and make it glow. If any attempt was made to move the lamp it would ignite the surrounding gas. When the conditions in a mine were wet, the resulting explosion would remain localised, badly burning and killing anyone in the vicinity. Should the mine be a dry mine (i.e. a mine free of water seepage), the sudden explosion and flash of methane would set off a chain reaction. The 'waft' of the explosion would lift the coal dust along the roadway and the flash would ignite it. The resulting explosion would roar along the mining galleries as if through an enormous gun barrel, burning and breaking men and materials alike, until it exhausted itself up the shaft with a report like a gigantic cannon. This is what happened at Moorfield Colliery on that November morning in 1883.

Davy discovered the principle of surrounding the flame with a cylinder of wire gauze, so fine that it would not allow the flame to pass through it to ignite the gas outside the lamp. This allowed lamps to be relatively light and easy to carry. With the introduction of safety lamps and improved ventilation, the miner was able to carry on working in a much gassier atmosphere. He would suffer from severe headaches and sickness of the stomach, but he would be able to carry on working and finish his shift without losing his light.

The three men refused to patent their individual inventions. When asked if he was going to cover his invention with a patent, Sir Humphrey replied: "*No, my good friend, I never thought of such a thing; my sole object was to serve the cause of humanity, and, if I have succeeded, I am amply rewarded in the gratifying reflection of having done so.*"

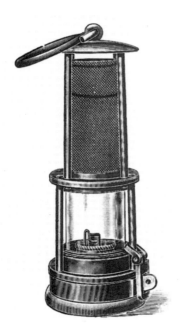

On the left the type of lamp used by the men at Moorfield, with an official's lamp on the right.

Over the years many attempts were made to improve the safety lamp, all using Davy's fine gauze principle. They all had one thing in common, *"they were lethal."* If the Davy Lamp was held in a current of air containing methane which was travelling at six feet (2m) per second or passed through a pocket of the same mixture, the flame would rise in the lamp. The gauze would become hot and glow like an old-fashioned gas mantle. In extreme cases the lamp itself would explode.

As the 19th Century progressed, better ventilation systems were introduced, allowing shafts to be sunk to a greater depth and mine workings to extend over a larger area. Within these deeper seams, methane, the curse of the miner, was to be found in greater quantities.

Coal dust: The essential ingredient.

It has often been asked why there was no mention of the coal dust at the inquest, but the answer is no mystery. The advance of mechanical haulage, and the movement of tubs along the roadways, resulted in the production of vast amounts of fine coal-dust. However, for many years, the danger of this coal-dust went unrecognised by the coal mining industry. When the danger was first brought up in the middle of the 19th century, it was disputed whether it did, or did not, contribute to mine explosions, and the argument went on for many years.

In 1844, the investigations of Michael Faraday revealed the part played by coal-dust in producing explosions. Dr. (later Professor) William Galloway, of Cardiff, continued experimenting in a search for the causes of colliery explosions. He stated that: *"It is coal-dust which carries the flame with disastrous effects along the roads of a colliery."* This conclusion was far from being in agreement with established theories and was so unpopular that he was forced to resign as a Junior Inspector of Mines. The Royal Commission of 1881, after forty years of evidence of the involvement of coal-dust in mine explosions, failed to reach a definite conclusion. Therefore insufficient attention was paid to the part played by the coal dust in the Moorfield explosion.

With the explosion at the Altoft Colliery in Yorkshire, and the loss of 22 lives in 1886 (three years after the Moorfield disaster), attention was once again focused on the danger of coal-dust.

William (later Sir William) Garforth, inspected the workings where the explosion had occurred and, from the evidence that he found, concluded that coal-dust had been the main cause of the explosion. To prove his theory, he built a section of enclosed mining galleries on the surface at Altoft Colliery, in which he carried out a series of experiments into the explosive properties of gas, coal-dust, and air mixtures. These experiments proved conclusively the explosive character of coal-dust/air mixtures, even in the absence of methane. Had this evidence been available at the Moorfield inquest, I believe there would have been a different culprit named for the deaths of the 68 men and boys, although the verdict would probably still have been the same.

Whinney Hill Colliery where the injured and dead were brought to the surface, as published in 'The Graphic', 17-11-83.

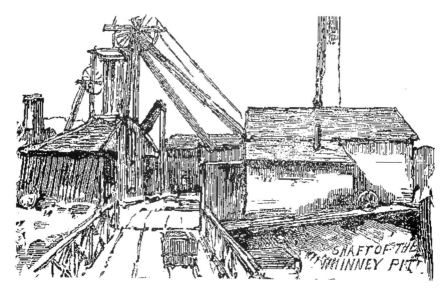

A view of the shaft mouth at Moorfield from the London Illustrated News.

Relatives identifying the dead at Whinney Hill Colliery,
a scene from 'The Graphic', 17-11-1883.

The Inquiry into the Moorfield Colliery Explosion.

15th, 16th, 21st and 22nd of November, 1883

The inquest was first held at the Greyhound Hotel, where the room was found to be too small. The venue was moved to the Hare and Hounds and then to the Mechanics' Institute, Clayton-le-Moors. The Coroner was Mr. H. J. Robinson, assisted by his clerk Mr. Wardle. Superintendent Eatough represented the police. The jury foreman was Joseph Walker, although the jury changed from day to day. There is a list of sixteen men sworn in as members of the jury, twelve of whom would be selected each day. The sixteen men were: Joseph Walker, the foreman; John Croasdale Kenyon; Henry Bretherton; Charles Dawson; Jacob Pilkington; Joshua Hacking; James Broadley; Sutcliffe Johnson; John William Briscall; Thomas Hargreaves; John Fletcher; James Wilson Bateson; William Green Marshall; Henry Leach Wilson; William Horrocks and John Greenwood.

The first death to be inquired into was not a direct victim of the explosion. It was to enquire into the death of Mr. John Frederick Seddon, manager of the Martholme Colliery. Mr. Seddon was a member of the rescue team. He had been underground for most of the day and was on his way home to Great Harwood. He accepted a lift in Dr. Cran's two wheeled carriage. On the journey the back-band broke and Mr. Seddon was thrown out onto the pavement, landing on his head. He had died instantly. The Jury returned a verdict of '*Accidental Death*'.

Mr. Smith, the undertaker, gave evidence that of the 61 men accounted for at this time, 37 had died from burns and injuries, 18 had been suffocated by 'afterdamp', 6 from burns only. Four had been brought out alive but had since died from the effects of burns and injuries.

The Evidence of William Swales, aged 15, drawer.

Mr. Arnold Morley, MP., representing the Home Office questioned Swales, who said:

> "*I was drawing for 'Tich', William Henry Mackerell, Billy Gumm, and my uncle James Broadley on No.2 level. I met a lad called John Mann who said his lamp had started blazing, and he said he could not blow it out. He said: 'I spit on it.' I said: 'Tha shouldn't ha done, tha should ha blowed it down.' Soon after my lamp started to fire. It was a blue flame, and it shot up when I was two to three yards further down than the 'points' between Bullock's end and the 'sheets'. It flashed and filled the lamp and then went down again. I said to Stephen Clough who I saw at Dick Bullock's end: 'I'll go and fetch Rushton at once.' The gas had extinguished Clough's lamp. Tim Yates (whose working place was filling with gas) came running out and telling others to come out of their places.*

Stephen Clough had his sledge with him. He said: 'Shine the leet, and I'll make it go.' So I got on with him and we both went out to N°. 2 level, and when we got to the Jig Road I said: 'I'll go down to Jack (John Rushton) and tell him.'"

On the way they met Thomas Henry Macintosh, the assistant fireman (no relation to Thomas Macintosh, the manager). He told them to hold on while he used his lamp to test for gas. At first there was little gas showing, then the flame in the lamp flared up. They told him that the gas was becoming so dense that it was driving out against the 'scale' of the fresh air coming in along the level. Swales caught up to Rushton at the bottom of the Jig Road, almost at the shaft.

"When I got to Jack, I said: 'Jack it's full of gas on yon level.' He said: 'How did it get on yon level? Some door tenters must have left a door open.'

'I heard Derry, (the nickname for Thomas Macintosh, the Manager) talking at the bottom of the Jig, and heard him say: 'What was that?' Peter Broadley answered the Manager, saying: 'He said there was gas on someone's level, but I did not hear whose level it was.'"

Rushton and the boy Swales went back up the Jig Road to N°. 2 District. Thomas Macintosh the Manager went through the air doors and up the travelling road. Broadley later told the enquiry: *'That was the last I saw of them.'*

Mr. J. Dickinson, Her Majesty's Chief Inspector of Mines, questioned Swales concerning the ventilation doors which the fireman Rushton had alleged had been left open. Swales explained:

"There was a door on the lower side of the N°. 2 level in the travelling road. The boy was told to keep the door shut and not to let loads of coal through. That door was to send the air on to the far end of N°. 2 District. I told him myself on account of the gas."

It would seem that on the way up the Jig Road, Rushton had told Swales to instruct the door tenter to keep the door shut, in an attempt to clear the gas off the district. Swales may have done this on his way out of the pit.

The Inspector then questioned him about events at the shaft bottom. Swales said:

"When I got to the shaft the 'getter' who were there kept telling Bickerstaff, the hooker-on, to knock up. Bickerstaff said he was waiting for a load of coal to fill the cage and when it had gone up the men could go up. He knocked the cage up, and the crack went off." (i.e. the explosion.)

It was ten minutes to nine. The blast heard by young William had come down the Jig Road and up the shaft damaging the cages and jamming them in the shaft, sealing it off as a means of escape. Any survivors now had to travel a thousand yards to the Whinney Hill shaft. Swales related how he was thrown a good distance by the blast, but was able to make his way up Billy Brow to the Whinney Hill shaft.

The search; a scene such as would have been found after the explosion. This illustration comes from a Victorian coalmining book.

"I was two or three yards from the shaft then. I got up and some lads seized me and said: 'Where are you going? Tha will fall into the dib hole.' I said: 'Nay let me alone. I can see where I'm going'. I went to the other side and groped about and found a door and got into the Billy Brow. I stuck to the bell wire for a time, but I kept falling down and I then crept up the centre."

The Evidence of Adam Gregory, aged 15, Drawer.

Gregory, of Back Burnley Road, Clayton-le-Moors, began a long session of cross-examination:-

"On the morning of Wednesday, 7th November I went to work at six o'clock. John Rushton was my fireman and he set me to work for Robert Rushton, Lawrence Rushton and Robert Gorton. I and William Rushton were the two drawers for these three getters who worked in the end straight up from the jig. It would be half-past eight when I saw John Almond. He was a getter and asked me if my getters were not coming out. I said: 'What for? What do you want 'em for?' He said there were gas'.

There were some more getters there, but I never looked at them. I went to the jig then and put on my clothes. I took my tub and ran down the 'jig road' to the bottom of the shaft and saw nothing more of my getters. I did not go back to them.

The hooker-on was a man called Bickerstaff who was also there. There were tubs of coal in the cage, which was full. I asked Bickerstaff to let me go up the pit, and so did the others. He replied: 'Derry (Thomas Macintosh, the Manager) said we had not to go up 'till he had sent word back or else came, and he went to see what there was.' I went to the other side of the shaft then, near the Billy Brow, and beside the cage. When I had been there about a minute, a shot blew off. I saw no fire but found myself in a tub. I was knocked down. Before, the tub would be about five or six yards behind me. My head was burnt, and my face and hands full of spots."

Mr. Dickinson, the Chief Inspector, pointed out that the lad's hair was singed. This was sixteen days after the accident.

Gregory went on to name some of the men and boys who were at the shaft bottom before the explosion, and said four of them went back into the workings again. They went along N°. 1 Level. They were going back to their getters, but did not get that far. *"When I got out of the tub I made my way to Whinney Hill."*

Cross-examined by Mr. Edgar, solicitor for the owners, Gregory said that the men who were with John on N°. 2 Level, seemed alarmed.

Edgar: *"You used the phrase. A shot blew off, what did you mean by it?"*
Gregory: *"It sounded like thunder."*
Edgar: *"You did not mean a shot was fired?"*
Gregory: *"It was an explosion. All the men and boys on the Billy Brow side of the shaft got out except one, and a good part of those on the other*

side were killed. The explosion was stronger on that side. It came down the Jig Road."

When asked about the presence of gas, Gregory said:

"I have been working here for about three years and have known there to be gas before. We have come out before on account of it. It was about six months since, but there was no explosion at that time. It was up on the level then. (The same road as the present case). We started work without leaving the pit."

Arthur Morley, MP., barrister-at-law instructed by the Solicitor to the Treasury, then questioned Gregory about events at the shaft bottom.

Morley: *"Can you remember exactly what Bickerstaff, the hooker-on said when he was asked to signal for the men to go up the pit?"*

Gregory: *"He said that Macintosh, the Manager, said we had not to go up the pit till he sent word, and he went to look what there was."*

Morley: *"Was the cage full of tubs of coal?"*

Gregory: *"Yes there were eight tubs full of coal."*

Morley: *"And did he immediately signal the pit top?"*

Gregory: *"About a minute afterwards. Perhaps about five minutes after I got to the shaft."*

Morley: *"What was he doing meantime?"*

Gregory: *"Stopping there."*

Morley: *"Did they just put the tubs in?"*

Gregory: *"They were in when I landed down."*

Morley: *"What was he waiting for with the cage full of coal?"*

Gregory: *"I don't know."*

At this point the Enquiry was adjourned to allow the Coroner and the jury to visit Bickerstaff at his own home where he was confined to bed due to his injuries. When questioned he said: *"I remember seeing the Manager. He left no orders with me."* Later when pressed he repeated: *"I had no orders from the Manager about sending men up till he gave the orders."*

The Enquiry was resumed at the Newsrooms of the Mechanics' Institute. Mr. Morley carried on with his cross-examination of Gregory.

Morley: *"You say that Bickerstaff knocked up and the cage came down and the explosion occurred?"*

Gregory: *"The cage had got halfway down when the explosion occurred, and the cage stuck in the shaft."*

Morley: *"From the time you got to the shaft the cage was only sent for once?"*

Gregory: *"That was all."*

Morley: *"What made you go round to the other side of the shaft?"*

Gregory: *"I don't know, I never used to go round to the other side."*

Morley: *"Did you think it was the safer side?"*

Gregory: *"It was the safer, but I did not know it was 'bown' to blow off.*

*There were some on the other side, and I went and joined them, I thought
I would go round to get a good place for getting the cage."*
Morley: *"Were you very much afraid yourself?"*
Gregory: *"No, but I should have been if I had known."* There was
laughter in the room at his answer.
Morley: *"You did not think there was going to be an explosion?"*
Gregory: *"No."*

It is here that I feel something should be said in defence of John Bickerstaff,
the hooker-on. It has always been the rule that when coal was being wound it was
tantamount to sacrilege for the winding to be stopped for any reason. Should a
man or group of men arrive at the shaft demanding to ride without a paper signed
by an official, it would be more than his job was worth for the hooker-on to interrupt
the winding of coal. The men have always been notorious for the antics and scams
they would pull to get up the pit on an early wind. Bickerstaff was probably only
trying to keep the men off his back when he said that the Manager had left orders
that they should not leave the pit till he sent word. Had he been aware of the
immediate danger there is no doubt he would have sent the men up the pit. To be
fair to the man he was only doing his job. When he was later questioned he freely
admitted he had not received any such orders. This must have took some courage
on his part when you remember that the only man who could have condemned
him as a liar, Thomas Macintosh, the Manager was dead. He must have had a
terrible time living with his own conscience and facing the local community.

The Evidence of James Macintosh, Manager of Whinney Hill Colliery.

*"I have been assistant at Whinney Hill to my father who was manager
for the Altham Colliery Company. I went down Whinney Hill Pit on the
morning of the explosion at Moorfield Pit at about half-past seven. The
ventilating furnaces for the two pits are at the bottom of the up-cast
shaft there. They were working properly and I noticed nothing unusual.
It was about quarter past eight when I returned to the surface, it would
be about a quarter to nine when the hooker-on at the bottom of the
downcast came to me on the surface. As a result of what he told me I
went down the pit at once, and saw after-damp coming from the return
airway from Moorfield."*

William Hope, the head fireman at Whinney Hill, had already given the order
to get their men out of the pit. Macintosh set off alone down the Billy Brow towards
the Moorfield shaft. He had travelled about two hundred yards when he was halted
by another cloud of after-damp. He returned to the Whinney Hill shaft and opened
a ventilation door to reduce the amount of air to the Whinney Hill workings. This
increased the pull on the return air from the Moorfield workings. Once again he
set off alone. About one hundred yards from the bottom of Billy Brow he met the
first of the survivors. The effects of the explosion had extinguished their lamps
and they were travelling in total darkness. After questioning them and assuring

them that help was on its way, he carried on with his journey to the Moorfield shaft bottom.

Arriving there he searched around and found twenty men, all of whom were either dead, burned or injured. All but two were on the west side of the shaft at the bottom of the Jig Road, down which the blast of the explosion had travelled. The survivors were in danger of being suffocated by the afterdamp and the dense smoke coming from a roll of brattice cloth which had caught fire.

Fifteen minutes after arriving on the scene he was joined by William Hope. Together they inspected the roadways around the area of the shaft and found that the ventilation doors on the north and west sides had been blown down. One double check door at the bottom of the Jig Road had been blown to pieces. The other, which opened by sliding into a recess, had been opened at the time of the explosion and was undamaged. The survivors had partly closed the door in an attempt to clear the afterdamp and smoke. They began to make what repairs they could to restore the ventilation.

On hearing shouts from someone on the N°. 1 West level, Hope went to investigate while Macintosh carried on with the repairs. When the ventilation current was moving again, Macintosh followed Hope along the level. He came across several bodies and Hope who was aiding those who were still alive.

Macintosh went further along the level and down through a cut-through to a roadway on the lower side where he found two men and a boy still alive. They had been working at the far end of the 'dip workings'. They had only felt what was described as a 'puff' and had carried on working until the afterdamp arrived. He brought them out to where there was clean gas-free air and took them to the shaft bottom.

The partial closing of the sliding door probably kept alive the survivors along the N°. 1 level. The diluting and diverting of the gas-laden air up the Billy Brow reduced the chances of recurring explosions.

Back at the shaft, one of the cages had been freed and was working again. The decision was taken to leave the bodies in the pit for the time being. Teams were formed to bring the bodies out of the workings to the shaft bottom. William Hope took charge of the recovery work, leading a team along N°. 1 level.

Once again James Macintosh set off alone. This time he went up the Jig Road towards the N°. 2 District. He must have known that his father must be somewhere in that district and that there was little or no chance of finding him alive. After passing several bodies, he reached the end of N°. 2 level at the top of the Jig Road. He found the level full of gas and could go no further. The brick stoppings between the Jig Road and Billy Brow, which were built to direct the air current along the N°. 2 level, had been blown down and the air was passing straight into Billy Brow, the return airway, without ventilating the N°. 2 district.

Macintosh set about repairing the damage by putting up tarpaulin screens to control the flow of air. Another of the Whinney Hill firemen, Robert Smithies, now joined him. Together they completed the work on the 'stoppings', thereby

Waiting for news: an illustration from a Victorian coalmining book.

restoring the ventilation. They made an attempt to go along the N°. 2 level, but after two hundred yards, they met more gas, and could go no further.

Not wanting to give up their search, they turned right down a cut-through to a lower level. Here they found six or seven sledges and decided to go on a board which ran in the same direction as the N°. 2 level. They found four bodies. Turning, they travelled back along the lower level, to a point where James Macintosh finally found his father. It would appear that he had been leading a group of fifteen men out of the workings, when the explosion had overtaken them. Several of the bodies were badly burnt: the rest had suffocated.

Unable to proceed, they returned the way they had come to the top of the Jig Road. Further help had now arrived and Macintosh instructed them to recover the twenty bodies they had found. Mr. P.W. Pickup, the owner of the Dunkenhalgh Colliery now joined Macintosh. A brattice sheet was erected along the higher side of N°. 2 level to boost the ventilation. This enabled them to get a distance of three hundred yards along the level as far as N°. 2 End, where they found two more bodies.

At this point James Macintosh told the enquiry: *"I went out after that."* It was 9 o'clock on the Thursday morning, over twenty four hours since he had descended the shaft at Whinney Hill. The rescue work was now well under way.

Rescue and Repair well under way ~ problems occur.

Up to this time the exploration had been made from Whinney Hill, but at about 4 o'clock in the afternoon the Moorfield shaft was repaired sufficiently for one of the cages to be worked. By 10 o'clock that night, most of those forming the first shift had left exhausted.

One of them, Mr. J. F. Seddon, the manager of Martholme Colliery, was thrown out of the carriage he was travelling home in and was killed. About this time, Mr. Martin, the Area Inspector of Mines, arrived and joined the explorers. A telegram summoned Mr. Dickinson, The Chief Inspector of Mines, from the Home Office. He arrived early on the Thursday morning, when the second shift was coming out. Having inspected the platform and landing plates, which had been blown upwards by the force of the explosion coming out of the shaft, he left the organisation of repair work to Mr. Macalpine, the colliery owner. He went below, accompanied by Mr. Martin and Mr. Pickup, the owner of Dunkenhalgh Colliery, both of whom had already spent considerable time underground with the search parties.

The broken tubs had been cast on one side in the Jig Brow and one line of tramway re-laid for the passage of tubs and riding sledges which were the only form of quick travelling in the low workings. Brick setters had commenced rebuilding the stoppings at one side of the Jig Brow and new air doors were being prepared.

By bratticing air forward and putting tarpaulin screens in the openings, steady progress was being made in dislodging the gas, pure methane. The return air, containing the displaced methane, was having to pass through the fires of the ventilating furnaces. This was the cause of some anxiety, in case the air and gas reached the fires mixed at the right proportions to be explosive. The flow of foul air was controlled at an air door, where fresh air was available to dilute it at some distance from the fires. The firedamp further in became difficult to move, and stood like a wall. The stoppings were rebuilt part of the way into N°. 2 Level, and doors set at the Jig Brow, which increased the air pressure. The gas, instead of moving into the return airway on the rise side, began to back out against the intake air in the level, passing the man placed in front for testing with the Davy lamp. The gas forced its way along the level, driving back the search party.

It was decided to move the men out of the district for two hours, and give the air a chance to clear the gas. The ventilation furnaces were checked, and after some discussion, it was decided to keep them lit. This would not have been an easy decision to make as there was tremendous risk involved. Should there be a sudden surge in the pressure of gas and it reached the furnaces undiluted, the resulting explosion would have totally destroyed the underground workings, killing everyone below ground. The force expelled from the shaft would have wrecked the headgear and killed anyone in the vicinity.

The Source is Found.

By Friday, the second day after the explosion, the main source of the gas was discovered. The roof had collapsed in two places at a small fault. At the innermost of these falls, gas was issuing with a noise like steam rushing through water. The issue of gas was more than the air could dilute. While the search was proceeding elsewhere it had to be left uncleared. Another issue, of a comparatively small quantity, was gurgling out from the same fault in the floor of a cut-through. The brick and mortar stopping had remained standing, while the stoppings in all of the other cut-throughs were blown out.

On Saturday, the third morning after the explosion, Mr. Dickinson, William Hope and Mr. John Higson, who had been called in by the owner, visited the far end of N°. 2 Level. They tried to clear the gas from the main blower but the issue was too strong for the air to clear. They could not approach the place where it was issuing except in the dark without their lamps. They also had to hold their breath to avoid being suffocated. The small blower was cleared through a vent in the stopping.

The gas from the large blower so fouled the return air in that part of the workings where the remainder of the bodies lay, that extra fresh air had to be diverted before the bodies could be recovered. The exhausting work went on, shift after shift. By Sunday, the fourth morning, the last of the bodies was reached and brought out. As far as trying to clear the blower would allow, the ventilation was then restored to its usual courses. On Tuesday 20th November parts of the mine were re-opened and forty getters returned to work.

The inquest came to an end on the Thursday 22nd November. The Coroner, in summing up, said he calculated that there were thirty-three men at the shaft bottom before the explosion took place. It was a pity that Bickerstaff, the hooker-on, did not take any notice of them. A suggestion had been made that the manager had given orders that no person had to leave; but Bickerstaff himself contradicted that. If he had sent up the men many lives might have been saved.

The jury retired for 30 minutes then returned their verdict:- *"We find the deceased Thomas Macintosh and others received certain injuries at Moorfield Pit, Altham, by reason of an explosion of gas on the 7th instant of which they died, either at the pit or at their own homes, that in the opinion of the jury the explosion was caused by a sudden outburst of gas, but how that was exploded there is no sufficient evidence to show."*

It was three weeks before there was any noticeable decrease in pressure from the 'blower'. Two months afterwards the load noise had ceased and the gas had become diluted a short distance from the source.

Shot firing at Moorfield.

There seems to be some doubt as to when shot firing was carried out at Moorfield. Under the Coal Mining Acts in force at the time, it was illegal to fire shots while other men were in the pit. John Waine gave evidence that William Yates was the only shotfirer and that shots where always fired before the miners entered the pit. He admitted that blasting powder was carried down at the same time as the first shift men. Why, if not to be used?

William Gregory contradicted this, saying he had heard shots fired after breakfast within the last three months. He also said: *"Many shots had been fired in the last six to seven months."* Asked how he knew, he replied that he had heard and smelt them. Whenever shots were fired in the pit a cloud of acrid smelling smoke would travel along the airways. Modern day explosives give off a strong smell of ammonia which is used as a flame depressant.

William Swales stated that he had heard shots being fired early in the morning, or just after breakfast, but not on the morning of the explosion. When asked, he told the inquest that he had heard shots being fired within 100 yards of the top of the Jig. He said they were fired by William Yates and James Obaldeston. He stated that he had heard shots being fired within the last week.

James Macintosh, the manager of Whinney Hill stated that shots were always fired before the men commenced work. He said that, as far as he knew, Yates and Wayne were the only shotfirers and that if there was a good amount of blasting it was carried out on the night shift.

The Question of Lamps: Some light is cast upon the subject.

Speculation and rumour were rife as to what had caused the explosion. There were several letters published in the local papers in the following weeks. Unfortunately, they are far too long to be included in this book. People with a coal mining background brought to the fore arguments aOs to the possible causes of the explosion and the advantages and disadvantages of the safety lamp.

At Moorfield, as at most other pits, the men cleaned and trimmed their own lamps at home. The lamps would be inspected before the men went down the pit. There were several ways in which the lamps could be locked, usually by using a copper rivet. It is not stated just how this was done at Moorfield, although it was probably by using a key. The firemen and the shotfirers were able to open their lamps with a key. It was illegal for an ordinary miner to open his lamp underground and risk an explosion. If caught in the act a man could by fined or imprisoned. With this in mind it was still common practice to open a lamp to re-light another's lamp. On the same day as the explosion, a miner at Aspen Colliery, Church, was found to be working with an open lamp. This was sometimes done to obtain a better light. He was later taken to court, where he said it was common practice at that particular pit. Aspen Colliery was a very wet pit, which reduced the chances of a large explosion. If a pocket of gas exploded it would be contained, the wet conditions would prevent the coal dust catching fire. He was fined 40s (£2) and costs, or a month's imprisonment in default of payment.

James Yates aged 16 of Church Lane-Ends was an assistant banksman at Moorfield. (It is not known if he was related to Tim or William Yates who were both killed). He told the inquest that on the morning of the explosion it was his job to inspect the miners' lamps before they descended the shaft. He did not inspect the firemens' lamps. They had already gone down the pit before he came to work. He said that all the firemen had keys including Wayne and Yates, to allow them to open their lamp to light the fuse when shotfiring.

John Bickerstaff, the onsetter, also had a key. This would not be unusual as the bottom of the downcast shaft would have been a designated lighting station. The area around the base of the shaft was illuminated by using open gaslights with glass chimneys, similar to those used in the houses of that time.

John William Thomson worked as a Jig tenter at the top of the Jig brow, but he was not working on the day of the explosion. He said that there was no lamp station at the top of the Jig brow, but he had a key and he had opened men's lamps when they had gone out and re-lighted them from his own. He said that he did this with the authority of the firemen and the manager.

All in all, it would seem that procedures at Moorfield were no different from any other colliery at that time. Terrible risks were taken and history reveals that the lives of thousands of men and boys were needlessly thrown away.

The Aftermath, and Organisation on the Pit Top.

The scene at the base of the Moorfield shaft immediately following the explosion must have resembled a scene from 'Dante's Inferno'; the injured calling for help as they lay in total darkness amongst the dead and dying. As they attempted to escape the suffocating afterdamp and choking smoke, several of the men and boys fell into the 'sump hole' below the shaft. Fortunately, all but one of them was rescued, mainly by the efforts of John Bickerstaff, the hooker-on.

Attempts were made to signal for the cage to be lowered, but the cage had been jammed in the shaft by the force of the explosion. The walking injured then began to make their way up the Billy Brow, to the Whinney Hill shaft, and on the way they were met by James Mackintosh, the manager at Whinney Hill.

The evacuation of the Whinney Hill men was already in progress. The hookers-on, William and John Pickup, had been driven out of the pit by the initial onslaught of afterdamp and smoke. Richard Wilton and others acted as hooker-on, and got the men and boys out of the pit.

Word soon spread and before long people began flocking to the pit, many of them the wives and mothers of those trapped below. Among these was William Rushton who had a grocer's shop close by. He had worked at the pit for nearly twelve years, retiring the previous summer due to poor health. Accompanied by two other local men, Alfred Marsden and Thomas Clough, he went down the pit to help in the rescue. On their way down Billy Brow, they met Thomas Hamriding and two or three boys. Hamriding declined their offers of help. He told them to go on, that there were others who needed help. He said he would make his own way out. He later died of his injuries. Rushton went as far as the Moorfield shaft from where he helped to bring out some of the injured. Not a well man himself, he then went home exhausted, leaving the rescue to younger and stronger men.

The owner, Mr. Macalpine, was on his way to work when he was informed of the explosion. He arrived at Moorfield and realising that nothing could be done there, drove to Whinney Hill and took charge of the rescue operation at the pit top. His wife and two female servants soon joined him. They brought with them bed linen and lint for dressings, and began to attend the injured as they were brought out of the pit. A nursing sister from Blackburn Royal Infirmary assisted them.

The two local doctors, Tattersall and Illingworth, managed the best way they could as the first batch of injured came out of the pit. Help arrived with Drs Geddie and Ruttle of Accrington. As the day drew on, Drs Milne and Dearden of Clayton, Dr. Monaghan of Accrington and Dr Lyons of Oswaldtwistle arrived at the colliery to render help.

As the injured were brought out, they were taken into the warmth of the engine house, where they were given hot sweet tea. Those fortunate enough not to be too severely injured had their wounds dressed and were sent home wrapped in blankets.

One of the men brought in was so badly burnt and disfigured that even the colliers were unable to identify him. Deep in shock he was unable to speak. One of the waiting women came forward and said: *"Yeah, that's Stevy Stepps"* (i.e. Stephen Clough). She was right. He later died of his injuries.

Samuel Halstead, when brought in, did not seem to be badly injured but he was in shock and very agitated and kept asking: *"Where am I?"* When told he asked: *"Oh! where's my boy?"* He was told: *"The boy's safe"*, and this seemed to calm him down.

At about 1.30pm winding ceased at Whinney Hill, as the last of the living were brought out. The day was bright, sunny and warm, a mercy to all those who stood and waited. As time went on, speculation went through the crowd that the rescue work had ended, and that only the dead remained below.

Several clergymen mixed with the crowd giving solace, taking names and addresses, with a promise that if only they would go home they would be sent word the instant there was any news,. The majority of the women preferred to wait. The police presence was limited to Sergeant Stroyan and P.C. Burns. The crowd grew larger as the afternoon passed. Police reinforcements arrived from Accrington and the County. When it was deemed advisable to clear the pit bank, Supt. Eatough took command of the operation.

Below ground, the bodies were being conveyed up the Billy Brow to the Whinney Hill shaft. The winding of the dead began about four o'clock. The first were laid out in the blacksmith's shop at the colliery. As each successive cage came to the surface the heart-rending sobs of the women could be heard above the sympathetic murmur of the crowd. The relatives were held back as each body was taken into the smithy. The bodies were laid out on boards about a yard off the floor and covered in white sheets.

Relatives identifying the dead. An illustration from 'The Graphic', 17-18-1883.

Their swollen and disfigured faces had to be washed and about twenty candles dimly lit the place. After a time, the relatives were admitted in twos and threes. One poor soul, arriving late and breathless, inquired if her husband was among them. On being told they had just brought him up, she completely broke down.

If the men recognised a body as they laid it out, they would inform the waiting relatives, who would then be taken in to formally identify it. There were sobs, wailing, and often piercing screams, as each corpse was identified. After a time the smithy could hold no more. Others were taken to a shed by the side of the Greyhound Inn, but this could only accommodate six bodies. A large wooden building at Bracewell's Timber Merchants, opposite the Greyhound, was then brought into use as a mortuary and all the corpses were transferred there.

About ten o'clock on the Thursday morning attempts were made to get the Moorfield shaft back in operation. A large bucket known as a hoppet was attached to a wire rope passing over a single pulley above the centre of the shaft. Thomas Woodhouse, the colliery blacksmith, with an assistant, was then lowered down to where the cage was jammed in the shaft. After several attempts, they freed the cage and it was lowered to the base of the shaft, where it was detached from the rope. The rope was then wound up and coiled onto the drum of the winding engine. The other undamaged cage was freed at 5.30pm. When it was deemed safe the rescuers went down at 8.00am to begin the gruesome task of winding up the remaining dead. The work of the recovery teams was now somewhat eased by not having to transport the dead on sledges up the Billy Brow. Councillor James Maden, a mason and builder, of Richmond Hill, Accrington, who had been working on the surface at Moorfield, took over the responsibility of despatching the bodies to the death house at Bracewell's yard. At one o'clock that night, the winding of the dead ceased for a time. Twenty-one bodies had been raised at Moorfield and eighteen at Whinney Hill. By late Friday evening, forty-four dead had been brought out, seventeen were still unaccounted for, and three of the injured had died at home. The last of the sixty men and boys killed in the mine were recovered on Sunday. Three of the men brought out alive had already died, and a further five were yet to die from their injuries.

Many of the bodies were so burnt they were beyond recognition. They had to be washed and cleaned before they could be viewed. Most of them could only be identified by their clothing or personal items found in their pockets. One of the men had a shilling and an orange in his pocket. His family kept them as a momento until the orange had dried and shrunk to the size of a walnut. One man did not realise he was washing the body of his own son until a friend pointed it out to him. Two women laid claim to the same body and it was only resolved by counting the number of false teeth the man possessed. One father, David Cronshaw, had the heart-breaking task of identifying and claiming the bodies of his three sons: James 27, Thomas 25 and Jackson 20. He also had another son, James H. Cronshaw who was badly injured. It was not uncommon in those days for children to share the same Christian name along with a middle name. What the initial H. stood for, and what name James usually used, I have been unable to trace.

THE VICTIMS

Name	Age	Name	Age
Almond, Cuthbert	12	Leeson, Joseph	12
Almond, John	20	Macintosh, Thomas	56
Alston, Thomas	16	Macintosh, Thomas Henry	35
Ashworth, James	39	Mackrell, William	21
Atherton, James.	10	Mahon, John	15
Bentley, John	32	Mahon, Michael	13
Blackburn, Thomas	23	Metcalf, Thomas	33
Broadley, James	40	Osbaldeston, James	37
Broadley, Westwell	28	Osbaldeston, Richard	12
Brown, Waddington Walter	23	Ormerod, John	41
Clegg, George	18	Perry, Mathew Henry	17
Clegg,, Henrey William	19	Riding, Aaron	10
Clough, James	27	Riley, Robert	17
Clough, Steven	19	Rushton, John	27
Coles, Walter Henry	32	Rushton, Lawrence	27
Crabb, John	40	Rushton, Robert	44
Cronshaw, Jackson	21	Rushton, William	14
Cronshaw, James	27	Scholes, James	19
Cronshaw, Thomas	25	Shorrock, John	19
Crossley, Henry	11	Smith, John Edward	11
Edge, John	16	Smith, Thomas	45
Edge, Thomas	14	Tapper, George	18
Gorton, Robert*	30	Taylor, James	35
Grimshaw, John	20	Taylor, Thomas	29
Grimshaw, Thomas	26	Taylor, William	24
Gumm, William*	26	Taylor, Wilson	29
Hall, John Thomas	15	Thornton, Joseph	24
Hamriding, Thomas	36	Threlfall, John	46
Haworth, Job Whittaker	11	Threfall, Robert	25
Haworth, Robert	36	Tillotson, Thomas	28
Haworth, Rothwell	34	Tomlinson, Peter	19
Haworth, William Henry	32	Walsh, Thomas	27
Hollin, William	25	Yates, Timothy	29
Jones, William Edward	13	Yates, William	46

* Robert Gordon. In the official list and on the memorial tablet, his name is given as Robert Gordon. His wife had his name registered in the Relief Fund register as Gorton. It is hard to define which is correct as his wife appears to have been semi-literate and the person who completed the form for her may not have realised the mistake. The records of the Registrar of Births, Marriages and Deaths show him as Gorton.

* William Gumm. On the list of dead, which was printed and sold to raise subscriptions, his name is given as William Gunns.

Almond, Cuthbert aged 12, of 10 Burnley Road, Clayton-le-Moors. A drawer, He was the brother of John, who was killed and George, who was injured.

Almond, John aged 20, of 10 Burnley Road, Clayton-le-Moors. A getter on N° 3 level. He was brought out injured and died the following Saturday. The brother of Cuthbert, who was killed and George who was injured. The two Almond boys were buried at Altham. Their brother George was also interred with them the following May .

A Lawrence Almond is listed as the father of the children in the Register of Births but it would appear Mrs. Almond was in fact a widow. Although some reports say she was left with six children, a claim signed by Ellen Almond was made on the Relief Fund for three: James b. 12-2-1874; Alice b. 11-5-1877; Catherine b. 27-11-1882, who died in July 1885; another daughter Mary Jane was 'of age'. (i.e. of working age)

The family moved to 21 Pleasant View St., Nelson in November the following year. They moved several times, first to 18 John St., Nelson, in December 1884, then to 11 Lower John St., in December 1885. In 1900, they were at 13 Ann St, Nelson, and their last address was 110 Smith St., Nelson.

There are several notations in the Relief Fund Register concerning the Almond family:

"Catherine Almond died July 1885 and £2/10/0d (£2-50p) was allowed, the child being illegitimate." This was half the amount that was usually granted on the death of a child. *"To be allowed 2/6 (12¹/₂p) to this date resolution October 22 1889."* *"This resolution was amended at a meeting held March 21 1890 when Mrs Almond was to be considered a widow and the 2/6 (12¹/₂p) was to be allowed to her in respect of this child Catherine who died."* *"At the meeting held September 23 1890, it was resolved to allow Mrs. Almond 5/- (25p) per week (from meeting to meeting only), until Alice arrives at the age of 15, then the allowance to be reduced to 2/6 (12¹/₂p) per week. Mrs. Almond being put in position of half a widow."* It is not clear what this means.

Alston, Thomas aged 16, of Church Lane Ends, Clayton-le-Moors. He was a drawer for James Clegg, and he was buried at Church Kirk.

Ashworth, James aged 39, of 8 Crawshaw St., Accrington. He left a wife Mary Ann, who was a cripple. She signed a statement dated 16th June 1884, *"My son was 13 years of age on the 22ⁿᵈ February 1884. I have never received any money on his account, as my late husband James Ashworth was his stepfather, so I thought it useless to fill up this form as he is over 13 years old."* She was allowed £1 per week from the fund. Mrs. Ashworth moved house several times. First to 33 Grange St., Accrington, then to 4 Cobden St., Accrington. She was living at 44 Paxton St., Accrington in 1899, 7 Crossedge, Oswaldtwistle in 1906, and 289 Burnley Rd., Rawtenstall, in 1907. It would seem that she never remarried and died in the Union Workhouse Haslingden, aged 78, on the 12ᵗʰ April 1919. James was interred at Accrington.

Atherton, James aged 10, of Petre St., Clayton-le-Moors. His brother was injured. At this young age, James would probably have worked as a door tenter. James was buried at All Saints, Clayton-le-Moors.

Bentley, John aged 32, of Edward St., Clayton-le-Moors. An address of 7 Canal Yard, Clayton-le-Moors, is also listed. He left a wife, Esther Ann, and five children: Amelia Anna b.16-3-1875; James b.7-11-1877; Sarah b.8-2-1879 (this date of birth was later amended to 8-2-1880) John b.8-4-1882. John's birth date was also contested and amended to 8-5-1882. Nickolas (so spelt in the Relief Fund Register) b.30-5-1884. Five months after the disaster. Mrs. Bentley married Albert Maundels in June 1887. John is interred at All Saints, Clayton-le-Moors.

Blackburn, Thomas aged 23, of 38 Walmsley St., Church. He left a wife Mary Alice and one child, Margaret Alice b.25-12-1882. The family later moved to 21 Ernest St., Church. Mary Alice remarried on the 12th January 1886 and moved to 10 Pearl St., Accrington. The family was living at 46 Maden St., Church in 1900. Mrs. Blackburn died on 5th Sept. 1924, aged 64. Thomas was interred at Church Kirk with John Shorrock who had been adopted by the Blackburn family.

Broadley, James aged 40, of Garden St., Oswaldtwistle. An address of 18 Hartley St., Oswaldtwistle is also given. He is listed in the Relief Fund Book as James Bradley of 18 Holly St., Oswaldtwistle. The brother of Westwell, he was a getter on No 2 level. He left a wife, Jane, and three children: Charlotte Alice b.18-12-1872, James Westwell b.17-6-1875; and David Parker b.11-1-1878. Mrs. Broadley died on 10th Dec. 1916, aged 77.

Broadley, Westwell aged 28, of 14 Edward St., Church. The brother of James, he left a wife Mary Ann, and one child Mary Alice b.1-9-1878. She married John Allman, of 117 Roegreave Rd., Oswaldtwistle, on 9th February 1885, and later moved to the Startled Fox beer house, 17 Union Rd., Oswaldtwistle. The Broadley brothers were buried at Church Kirk.

Brown, Waddington Walter aged 23, of 9 Ernest St., Church. An address of 23 Market St., Church, is also listed. He left his wife Mary Jane, and one child, Susannah, 12-9-1882. He was one of the last to be brought out on the Sunday. Mrs. Brown was married on September 13th 1884 to a person named Grimshaw. Walter was buried at Church Kirk.

Clegg, George aged 18, of 15 Wade St., Church. A drawer. The brother of William, he left a wife Elizabeth Ellen, who moved to 12 Water St., Church, in October 1885. George was buried at Church Kirk. Elizabeth died on 8th February 1892.

Clegg, William Henry aged 19, of 15 Wade St., Church. The brother of George. His father, James Clegg, was helping to wash the bodies in the smithy at Whinney Hill. He had washed the face of one man and moved on, when a neighbour recognised it and said: *"That's Jim Clegg's son."* He checked the body again and said: *"Nay, that's noan our William Henry."* Mrs. Clegg was brought in. On opening the shirt, she recognised a scar on the chest where she had applied a mustard plaster. Mrs Clegg also lost two brothers.

James Clegg had been legally separated from his wife for a number of years. On the Sunday night after the funeral, he turned up at the house where his other son, Thomas, was lying injured. He was drunk and demanded money from his wife. The police were called and he was arrested. In court the following day, it was found that there was already a warrant out for his arrest, for a separate offence. He was sentenced to fourteen days on each charge, in default of paying a fine. Both the Clegg boys were buried at Church Kirk.

Clough, James aged 27, of Quarry St., Clayton-le-Moors. An address of Well St., and one at High St., Clayton-le-Moors are also listed. He left a wife Eliza and two children: Anne b.24-8-1881 and Ellen b.2-9-1882. Another child, Eliza, was born on the 2nd July 1884, nine months after the disaster. Mrs. Clough was remarried, on the 13th May 1886, to William Haworth. James was buried at All Saints, Clayton-le-Moors.

Clough, Stephen aged 19, of 65 Napoleon St., Clayton-le-Moors. He was a drawer. He had a fractured skull and was so badly burnt he could not be identified, until one woman viewing the body said: *"Yeah that's Stevey Stepps"*. Stephen was interred at All Saints, Clayton-le-Moors.

Coles, Walter Henry aged 32, of 37 Queen St., Clayton-le-Moors. He left a wife Jane and six children; Elizabeth Jane b.5-4-1875, who died on 31-7-1885; William b.13-12-1876; James b.7-4-1879; he died 12-7-1885, Mary b.4-7-1880; Henry, 2-3-1882; and Joseph b.22-11-1883 (fifteen days after the disaster). Mrs. Coles later married Henry...?

Henry Coles was a bandsman in the local Volunteer Corps, a forerunner of the Territorial Army, and was given a military funeral. The procession from his home, to St. Mary's Catholic burial ground at Altham, was led by a twelve man firing party, under the command of Colour Sergeant Seddon. The Corps band playing the 'Dead March' and then followed by the flag-draped coffin, carried by four members of the Corps followed by four relief men. Behind, marched forty-two officers and men from G and H Companies. Due to a late arrival, and five other burials, the funeral was held up for two hours on a cold wet day. Three volleys were fired over the grave and the band played 'The Last Wish'. On the return from the graveyard they marched to the tune 'The Gloria' by Mozart.

Crabb, John aged 40, of 72 Pickup St., Clayton-le-Moors. John and his wife Elizabeth had no children and she remarried on Whit Monday 1885. His funeral was an impressive affair. John was a staunch Wesleyan and Sunday school teacher. He was also a member of the Rechabites and the Blue Ribbon Order. A large number of members, from both lodges, preceded the coffin with a group of his Sunday school pupils following behind. They formed a large procession to his interment at All Saints, Clayton-le-Moors.

Cronshaw, Jackson aged 21, of Church Lane, Clayton-le-Moors. The brother of James and Thomas, his was one of the last bodies to be recovered on the Sunday.

Cronshaw, James aged 27, of 23 Napoleon St., Clayton Le Moors. James left a wife Elizabeth Ann, and three children: Lily b.11-2-1879; Mary Jane b.31-3-1881; and

David, first registered as b.5-9-1883, but this was later amended to 5-9-1882. Mrs. Cronshaw was remarried on the 15th December the following year, to Henry Cunliffe, of Church Lane.

Cronshaw, Thomas aged 25, of Church Lane, Clayton-le-Moors. The Cronshaw brothers are buried at Altham, although not in the same grave.

This was not the first time tragedy had struck the Cronshaw family. They had already lost one son in a mining accident. Another son was drowned in the local canal, and, in the previous twelve months, they had buried their daughter Jane. David Cronshaw, the father, had suffered the heart-breaking task of identifying the bodies of his three sons. Another son, James, was injured in the explosion. The family later moved to Burnley. Mr. Cronshaw survived his sons by six short years. He passed away in 1889, aged 58, closely followed by his wife Ann, on the 28th August 1890, aged 51, She was interred with her son Thomas.

Crossley, Henry aged 11, of 3 Hart St., Accrington. A door tenter, he died on the morning of his third working day. Identified by his mother. Henry was buried at Accrington.

Edge, John aged 16, of 36 Lower Barnes St., Clayton-le-Moors. A drawer, he was the brother of Thomas.

Edge, Thomas aged 14, of 36 Lower Barnes St., Clayton-le-Moor. He was the brother of John. A drawer, he was badly injured and was carried out of the pit by his father. Tom never regained consciousness and died in Blackburn Infirmary on the following Monday. The two young boys were buried at Saint Bartholomew's Church, Great Harwood.

Gorton, Robert aged 30, of 37 Henry St., Clayton-le-Moors. A getter on N°. 3 level. In the register Robert's wife gives her name as Alice Gorton. She had made some attempt at filling in the details but it would seem since she was almost illiterate someone else completed the task and the name written along side her mark X was Alice Gorton. She claimed for herself and two children; Mary Elizabeth b.8-12-1877; and George b.1-3-1880. An address is given at 27 Perseverance St., Oswaldtwistle, for January 1885. Alice married Robert Fielding on 25th January 1886, and they moved to the Stanhill Inn, Oswaldtwistle.
Robert Gorton was buried at Immanuel Church, Oswaldtwistle. In one record, he is shown as Robert Gordon.

Grimshaw, John aged 20, of 81 Henry St., Church. He was one of the last four to be recovered on the Sunday. He may have been living with his grandparents. On the death of his grandfather, William, in October 1895, his grandmother was classed as a widow and began to receive support from the fund. John was buried at the Wesleyan Church, Mount Pleasant, Oswaldtwistle.

Grimshaw, Thomas aged 26, of Church Lane, Clayton-le-Moors. He left a wife, Agnes, and a daughter, Nancy Alice b.9-6-1882, who was listed in the Relief Fund Register as Agnes. The child died 2nd December 1885 aged three. The family later moved to 37 Union Rd., Oswaldtwistle. Mrs. Grimshaw married John Hughes, of Church Lane, on 15th December 1884. Thomas was buried at the Wesleyan Church, Mount Pleasant, Oswaldtwistle.

Gumm, William aged 25, of 7 Arnold St., Accrington. An address of 20 Croft St., Accrington, is also listed. He was a getter on N°. 2 level. He survived the explosion only to die later of his injuries. Billy left a wife Elizabeth and four children: Elizabeth Hannah b.8-10-1878; William Henry b.12-1-1880; Joseph b.13-1-1882 and James who was born three months after the disaster, on 16-2-1884. The family later moved to 34 Adelaide St., Accrington, and then to 40 Chapel St., Accrington, in 1887. The mother died in May 1888. For a short time a Mrs. Rose Hannah Stockdale looked after the family before being split up. The two elder children went to live with Mr. Richard Leach, at 163 Higher Antley St., Accrington. "*Allowance of 5/- (25p) stopped Oct. '95*", (no reason was given). William later went to live with Thomas Mason at Laund Farm. Joseph went to live with James Gumm of Annie St., Accrington and James to James and Nanny Slater of Culvert St., Accrington. William was buried at Accrington. In one record, William is shown as Gunns.

Hall, John Thomas aged 15, of 42 Commercial Road, Great Harwood. An address of 76 Lower Barnes St., Clayton-le-Moors, is also listed. A drawer, his parents had separated and it seems that John supported his mother, although he did have an older brother who identified his body. His mother was awarded 5/- (25p) per week from the Relief Fund. Mrs. Hall died 13th April 1891. John was buried at All Saints, Clayton-le-Moors

Hamriding, Thomas aged 36 of 69 Henry St., Clayton-le-Moors. He left a wife Ellen (or Ann) and four children: Margaret Alice b.23-9-1873; Jane Ann b.8-10-1875; James b.25-7-1878 and Mary, b.10-3-1881. Thomas had a son injured in the explosion, but I have been unable to trace his name. Mrs. Hamriding remarried 6th April 1890. Thomas was buried at All Saints, Clayton-le-Moors.

Haworth, Job Whittaker aged 11, of 33 Bates St., Clayton-le-Moors. Probably a 'trapper boy' or door tenter. The brother of Rothwell. In 1898, his mother, then aged 60, was allowed 2/6 (12½p) per week from the fund. Job was buried at All Saints, Clayton-le-Moors.

Haworth, Robert aged 36 of Church Lane End, Altham. The brother of William Henry. He left a wife Mary Ann and two sons: Robert b.17-12-1879 and John William b.16-3-1883. The family later moved to 7 Bismarck St., off New Lane, Oswaldtwistle, then again to White Ash Lane, Oswaldtwistle. Mary Ann married to John Bowker on the 10th Sept. 1897. Robert was buried at Immanuel Church, Oswaldtwistle.

Haworth, Rothwell aged 34, of 4 Church Lane, Clayton-le-Moors. He was the brother of Job. He left a wife Susannah, who was said to be "*in a feeble state*", and five children: Sarah Ellen b.28-2-1874; John James b.27-4-1876; George b.16-10-1877; Ann b.1-5-1881 and Catherine b.14-9-1883, who was only a little over seven weeks old when her father was killed. The family later moved to 3 White Ash Lane, Oswaldtwistle. Mrs. Haworth was married on the 21st December, 1884 to Richard Grimshaw. Rothwell was buried at Immanuel Church, Oswaldtwistle.

Haworth, William Henry aged 32, of Napoleon St., Clayton-le-Moors. The brother of Robert, he left a wife Alice and three children: Mary Ellen b.28-10-1872; Joseph William b.20-7-1879 and Alice Ann b.10-10-1882 who died aged five on 2nd January 1888. The family moved several times over the years. First to 15 Vine St., Oswaldtwistle, then in 1900 to 17 C...St., Church, in 1904 to 15 Back Stone Row, Foxcroft, Clayton-le-Moors and in 1906 to 6 Church St., Oswaldtwistle. Mrs. Haworth died 18th May 1924 aged 71. William was buried at the Baptist Church, New Lane, Oswaldtwistle.

Hollin, William aged 25, of 23/28? Garden St., Oswaldtwistle. He left a wife Harriet and two children: George b.9-11-1879 who died on 5th July 1884, and Alice b.5-8-1882. Harriet married William Barnes on the 14th Feb. 1885 and moved to 22 Garden St., Oswaldtwistle. William was buried at Immanuel Church, Oswaldtwistle.

Jones, William Edward Peacoup aged 13, of 92 Lower Barnes St., Clayton-le-Moors. He was brought out badly burned and crushed, he also had a fractured skull. He died on the Friday afternoon. His mother said that he had been constantly calling out. *"Thunder-thunder, fire-fire, wind me up"*. The location of William's resting-place is unknown.

Leeson, Joseph aged 12, of Waterloo St., Clayton-le-Moors. Being so young he was probably a door tenter. A 'half-timer' he was identified by his father. Joseph was buried at Saint Mary's burial ground, Altham.

Macintosh, Thomas aged 55 of Whinfield Terrace, Clayton-le-Moors. A widower and father of three. He had been the colliery manager since the pit opened in 1869. An award was made to a John Macintosh, his son, *"until he is in receipt of wages"*. From March 1884 he was awarded £15 per year until he completed his apprenticeship. The last payment was made in July 1886. Thomas was buried at Altham. He was nicknamed 'Derry' by the miners.

Macintosh, Thomas Henry 35, of 8 Edward St; Church. 1 Church Lane, Clayton-le-Moors is also listed. He was an assistant fireman to John Rushton on 1 and 2 districts. He left a wife Ann Mary, who it was said *"was a feeble woman"* and one son Thomas Henry b.26-7-1877. Ann Mary married Amos Renshaw, of 58 Dill Hall Lane, Church, on 10th October 1890. Thomas Henry was buried Church Kirk.

Mackrell, William Henry aged 21, of 12 Croft St., Accrington. Known as 'Tich' to his mates, he was a getter on the N°. 2 level. He left a wife Alice and two children. Alice b.21-8-1871 and John b.6-4-1878. The family later moved to 31 Derby St., Accrington on 15-1-1885, then to 2 Buxton St., Accrington in 1899 and to 16 Victoria St., Accrington in 1904. Mrs. Mackrell died 12th Jan. 1915. William was buried at Accrington.

Mahon, John aged 15, of 13 Lower Barnes St., Clayton-le-Moors. A drawer, the elder brother of Michael. When his lamp flared up he had tried to put it out by spitting on it. His mother identified him. She moved to Victoria St., Clayton-le-Moors in 1906 and died 26th May 1923 aged 82. An address in Super St., Clayton-le-Moors is also listed.

Mahon, Michael aged 13, of Super St., off Lower Barnes St., Clayton-le-Moors. Michael survived the explosion and was on his way out of the pit. He was half way up Billy Brow when he turned back to search for his brother. He was later found suffocated by the 'afterdamp'. The Mahon boys were buried in Saint Mary's burial ground Altham.

Metcalf, Thomas aged 33 of Old Engine House, Altham. A dataler. He left a wife Elizabeth and four children: Herbert b.13-9-1875; James Marshall b.30-9-1877; Maud b.28-8-1879 and Sarah b.31-8-1881. The family later moved to Bank Terrace, Altham. Mrs. Metcalf married on 21th January 1886 to George Hudson, a quarryman from Huncoat. Thomas was buried at Altham.

Osbaldeston, James aged 37, of 7 Well St., Rishton, an address of Quarry St., Clayton-le-Moors is also listed. Originally from Preston, James worked as a dataler. He left a wife Sarah and two daughters: Sarah Elizabeth b.6-11-1878 and Mary Ann b.22-9-1883. Their son Richard was brought out of the pit injured but later died. His nephew identified James. His wife was unable to attend the inquest., The family moved to 7 J......St., Clayton-le-Moors in 1906 and then 7 Quarry St., Clayton-le-Moors, in 1907. Mrs Osbaldeston died 13th June 1911 aged 70. Father and son were buried at Accrington.

Osbaldeston, Richard aged 12. The only son of James who was also killed. He was brought out of the pit badly burnt and later died at home on Thursday 15th November. His address was given as 7 Quarry St., Clayton-le-Moors.

Ormerod, John aged 41, of 80 Barnes St., Clayton-le-Moors. A single man, John was '*sole support to two sisters who both have fits*', Ann, also known as '*Nanny*', aged 45 and Alice, aged 37. Alice died the 5th October 1886 and £5 was allocated from the fund to have her interred with her brother. Payment from the fund was reduced from 7/6 (37p) to 5/- (25p) in Oct. 89. (no reason given). Over the years two large medical bills were paid from the fund, £7.16.0 (£7.80p) was paid to Dr. Tattersall, and £14 was paid to Dr. Patchall in Feb. 1889. Ann died 25th May 1895. A burial grant of £5 was paid from the fund. John was buried at Saint Mary's burial ground, Altham.

Perry, Matthew Henry aged 17, of 18 Wade St., Church. A married man with no children. When the bodies were routinely searched a pipe containing tobacco and three matches were found in his coat pocket. Although it was strictly against the law it was not uncommon in those days for a man to sneak a smoke in places which were considered safe, e.g. the base of the downcast shaft. His widow Nancy died 24th August 1888. Matthew is buried at Church Kirk.

Riding, Aaron aged 10, of Henry St., Clayton-le-Moors. A door tenter. His mother was awarded 3/- (15p) per week, which was discontinued in Oct. 1889. Aaron was buried at All Saints, Clayton-le-Moors.

Riley, Robert aged 17, of 120 Napoleon St., Clayton-le-Moors. An orphan, Robert was buried at Immanuel Church, Oswaldtwistle.

Rushton, John aged 27, of 34 Church Lane, Clayton-le-Moors. Addresses of 10 High St., Clayton-le-Moors and Church St., Church are also listed. John was the fireman assisted by Thomas Henry Macintosh, in charge of numbers 1 and 2 districts. He died from severe head injuries. He left a wife Mary and four children. Thomas b.6-5-1878; Richard b.7-11-1879; Elizabeth Ann b.7-11-1881 and Henry b.21-8-1883. His wife moved to 4 Church Lane, Clayton-le-Moors on 22nd May1885 and was married to Joseph Massland? on 6th May 1886. John was buried at Church Kirk.

Rushton, Lawrence aged 27 of Moorside, Altham. He was a getter on N° 3 district. His wife remarried and died 21-1-1894. He had a daughter Susannah who, on becoming 13 yrs, was ineligible for benefits from 1- 8-1895. Lawrence was buried at Altham.

Rushton, Robert aged 44, of Henry St., Clayton-le-Moors. He was a 'getter' on the No 3 level. His nickname at the pit was '*Crash*'. The father of William who was also killed. Robert's body was the last to be recovered on the Sunday. He left a wife, Theresa, and five children. Sarah who was over thirteen and could not make a claim from the fund: Alice b.26-9-1870, who was also of age at the time of the claim and was disallowed; twins, Ellen and Edward b.1-3-1878; and Gilbert b.2-11-1881. There is a note in the register dated Feb. 1888, '*increase 2/6 for 3 months sickness*'. The family moved twice, first to 2 Tremellen St., Accrington, in 1898, then to 23 Lister St., Accrington, in 1906. Mrs. Rushton died on the 28th March 1909. Robert and his son William were buried at Immanuel Church, Oswaldtwistle.

Rushton, William aged 14, of 25 Henry St., Clayton-le-Moors. The son of Robert Rushton, who was also killed. He was a drawer on N°. 3 level

Scholes, James aged 19, of 63 Napoleon St., Clayton-le-Moors. A single man, he worked as a drawer. James was buried at Immanuel Church, Oswaldtwistle.

Shorrock, John aged 19, of 33 Maden St., Church. John, an orphan, was adopted by the family of Thomas Blackburn. John and Thomas were buried together at Church Kirk.

Smith, John Edward aged 11, of 45 Henry St., Clayton-le-Moors. A 'short time' door tenter. Identified by his mother, he was buried at Altham.

Smith, Thomas aged 43 of 2 Hygiene Place, Clayton-le-Moors. Left a wife, Ellen, and seven children, two of whom were 'of age' and not listed in the Relief Fund register. The others were Margaret b.18-6-1873; Clara b.24-7-1875; Mary Elizabeth b.15-11-1877; Ellen b.2-2-1880 and a son James b.19-5-1882. His wife remarried in February 1887. Thomas was buried at All Saints, Clayton-le-Moors.

Tapper, George aged 18, of 70 Burnley Road, Accrington. A drawer. A single man living at home with his mother, a widow with ten children. George is buried at Accrington.

Taylor, James aged 39 of 4 Havelock St., Oswaldtwistle. An address of 4 Canal Yard, Clayton-le-Moors is also listed. A getter, he was known to his mates as '*Jim o' Tolls*'. James was buried at Immanuel Church, Oswaldtwistle.

Taylor, Thomas aged 32 of 23 Garden St., Oswaldtwistle. He left a wife Elizabeth Ellen, and two children: Alice b.11-6-1876 and James b.22-10-1882. Mrs. Taylor married William …? in December the following year. The family then moved house twice, to 20 Sun St., Oswaldtwistle, in March 1885 and to 28 Garden St., Oswaldtwistle, in May 1905. Thomas was buried at Immanuel Church, Oswaldtwistle.

Taylor, William aged 23 of Edward St., Clayton-le-Moors. He left a wife, Sarah Alice. They had no children. His body was one of the last to be recovered and was identified by his father. Mrs Taylor, who it seems was off work due to illness, was awarded 7/6 (37$^{1}/_{2}$p) per week until she was fit for work. She married Henry Pomfret on 16th August 1889. William was buried at Immanuel Church, Oswaldtwistle.

Taylor, Wilson aged 29, of 7 Chapel St., Accrington. He left a wife Charlotte, and three children: Harriet Ann b.28-3-1881; Thomas b.4-7-1882;and Martha, who was born seven months after the explosion, on 18-6-1884. The family later moved to 1 Hargreaves St., Accrington. Mrs. Taylor died and was buried on 4th April 1885. The children went to live with their grandparents Thomas and Hannah Taylor, at 38 Adelaide St., Accrington. The grandfather died in July 1892, the grandmother on 12-8-1894. The children then went to live next door at 36 Adelaide St., with their aunt and uncle, Ann and Matthew Ashworth. Wilson was buried at Accrington.

Thornton, Joseph aged 24, of Napoleon St., Clayton-le-Moors. Recently married, he left a wife Agnes, they had no children. Mrs. Thornton moved to Waterloo St., Clayton-le-Moors, in 1906. She died on 11th June 1926 aged 70. Mrs. Thornton was the last dependant paid from the Relief Fund. Joseph was buried at Accrington.

Threlfall, John aged 46, of Victoria St., Clayton-le-Moors. The father of Robert, he left a wife, Ann and two children: John b.24-6-1872 and Jane Ann b.23-7-1876. Mrs. Threlfall died on the 19th January. 1895. He was buried at Saint Mary's burial ground, Altham with his son Robert.

Threlfall, Robert William aged 25, of Queen St., Clayton-le-Moors. The son of John, he left a wife Alice Ann, and two children: William Edward b.6-6-1882 and Clara Ann, who was born fourteen days before her father was killed. Mrs. Threlfall remarried on 8th May 1895.

Tillotson, Thomas aged 28, of 60 Annie St., Accrington. He left a wife Mary Jane, and a daughter Bertha b.11-12-1881. He is also listed as being the father of two other children who may have been 'of age'. A death grant of £2 was paid out in May and a further £3 in June of 1884 but it is not clear for whom they were paid. The family later moved to 54 Water St., Accrington and then in 1900, to 9 Stanley St., Accrington. Mrs. Tillotson died 31st May 1901. Thomas was buried at Accrington.

Tomlinson, Peter aged 19, of 35 Henry St., Clayton-le-Moors. A single man, Peter was buried at Immanuel Church, Oswaldtwistle.

Walsh, Thomas Alfred aged 27, of 47 Henry St., Oswaldtwistle. Two years earlier the family was living at 21 Quarry St., Clayton-le-Moors. An address in Napoleon St., Clayton-le-Moors, is also listed. He left a wife, Sarah Jane, and two children: Elizabeth Ellen b.21-1-1881 and William b.4-9-1883, less than one month prior to the disaster. Thomas had a home industry making 'Turkey Red' dye. He was probably not a full-time miner but he had been asked to go in on the day of the explosion.

There is a note in the Pay Book, dated June 1884, stating that the family moved to Radcliffe then moved back again. Mrs. Walsh was married on 22nd December, 1884 to William Thomas Anderton, the man who brought Thomas' body out of the pit. They had three children Lily, Jim and Alice. Thomas was buried at All Saints, Clayton-le-Moors.

Yates, Timothy aged 29, of 8 Church Lane, Clayton-le-Moors. A shotfirer, he was driving a cut-through between two levels. He turned away offers of help, saying he would make his own way to the shaft. He came out of the pit alive but died on the morning of Friday 16th November. He left a wife, Mary, and three children: Ada b.2-9-1878; Sarah Jane b.31-7-1880 and Albert b.26-8-1882. The family moved to Blackburn, first to 13 Frederick Row, Furthergate, and then to the home of Mary's father, Robert Trotter, 31 Artillery St., where Mary died on the 27th July 1888. Mary's death must have been anticipated, for Timothy's brother, James, became the guardian of Ada and Albert on the 12th July, fifteen days before she died and they went to live at 101 Oxford St., Burnley. On the same day Timothy's other brother Roger became the guardian of Sarah Jane. Timothy's resting-place is unknown.

Yates, William aged 46, of 8 Clayton St., Clayton-le-Moors. A 'dataler'. He left a wife, Sarah, and nine children, six of whom are listed in the Relief Fund Register. (The others, the eldest being eighteen, would be of age) James b.14-7-1871; Mary Ellen b.5-11-1873; Sarah b.4-5-1876; Alice b.11-11-1878; Elizabeth b.1-6-1881 and Agnes b.1-3-1883. Mrs Yates married George Clegg, on 3rd September, 1887. William was buried at All Saints, Clayton-le-Moors.

THE INJURED

Almond, George of 10 Burnley Road, Clayton-le-Moors. The brother of Cuthbert and John who were both killed. George died in May 1884 at a hospital in Buxton, Derbyshire. He died from an overdose of chloroform while having a tooth extracted. There is a notation in the Pay Book that £6/16/0d (£6.80p) expenses were paid to Mr. Macalpine for bringing back his body. He was interred with his brothers at Altham.

Aspden, William Thomas of Quarry St., Clayton-le-Moors.

Atherton, Ben. A boy, the brother of James Atherton who was killed. (Age and other details are unknown).

Balderston, Richard, S. of Quarry St., Clayton-le-Moors. A Boy. (Age and other details are unknown).

Bickerstaff, John of Chequers, Clayton-le-Moors. The onsetter, he was blown into the sump at the base of the shaft by the force of the explosion. He helped in the rescue of the others who had also been blown into the sump. He was badly injured and was confined to bed. When his evidence was needed the coroner and the jury visited him at home, a small toffee shop, and had to stand around his bed in the cramped bedroom.

Bradley, David. Lived at 10 Stone Bridge, Oswaldtwistle, in 1900, when he made a claim on the fund. In 1906 he was living at 233 Union Rd., Oswaldtwistle. There was a claim made for two children, Charlotte Alice b.18-12-72 who came of age 18-12-1885, and James who was listed in the accounts for 4th September 1885. He was the uncle of William Swales.

Broadley, Peter, Church Lane, Enfield. He had previously worked at Cock Bridge (Martholme) Colliery. He was a fireman but was illiterate, unusual in a job with so much responsibility. He would make his inspection of his district and report to John Rushton who would write down the details. He gave evidence that he had been blown off his sledge. He injured his knee when he jumped into the sump hole to help in the rescue of the injured. A claim was made for a daughter Margaret Ann b.1.9.78.

Clegg, Thomas of 15 Wade St., Church.

Clough, John of Napoleon St., Clayton-le-Moors. The 'Jig tenter' on the Jig brow. He gave evidence that he often opened his lamp to re-light other men's lamps that had been accidentally extinguished. The top of the Jig brow was not a designated 'lighting station'. This was not only illegal but very dangerous.

Clough, William aged 18, of Napoleon St., Clayton-le-Moors (married). He made a claim for support on 19th May 1910 and was allowed 2/6 (12½p) per week. On the 29th June 1914, he was admitted to the Lunacy Ward at Blackburn Union Workhouse, aged 48.

Cronshaw, James H. of Well St., Clayton-le-Moors (a youth).

Crook, Edward George of High St., Clayton-le-Moors. He returned to work in July 1884.

Crook, James of High St., Clayton-le-Moors. A Boy.

Crossley, Henry of 3 Hart St., Accrington.

Duckworth, Joseph of Wellington St., Clayton-le-Moors.

Duckworth, Thomas of Bailey St., Enfield (a single man).

Fielding, James aged 19, of 30 Well St., Clayton-le-Moors, or 36 Henry St., Clayton-le-Moors, a married man.

Grace, William aged 12, of 27 Henry St., Enfield. He suffered from being gassed. In August 1903, he was living at 29 Unity St., Rishton. A Mrs Bolton made a claim on the fund for his support. By 1906 he was living at 29 Chapel St., Rishton. He then moved to 130 High St., Rishton. For the next two years, his pension was signed for by a Jane Grace? On the 18th September 1909 at the age of 37 he was admitted to the Whittingham Asylum.

Grace, Thomas of Henry St., Clayton-le-Moors.

Greaves, Thomas of 27 Henry St., Clayton-le-Moors.

Gregory, Adam aged 15, of Burnley Rd.? A drawer.

Grimshaw, William of Church. Died 8 August 1894. Someone made a claim for relief and was awarded 5/- (25p) per week. This was stopped in October 1889, reinstated at 2/6 (12½p) and increased in 1895.

Guilfoil, John. No further details known.

Gumm, Chris of 20 Croft St., Accrington. A drawer for Lawrence Metcalf. He told the inquest that when he saw light at a distance he climbed into an empty tub.

Gumm, Timothy of 20 Croft St., Accrington. A drawer.

Halstead, Samuel Church Bridge, or Back Henry St., Church (married).

Heap, Richard. He made a claim for someone named Mary Ann and was awarded 5/- (25p) per week. This was discontinued in October 1898.

James, Eli William of Lower Barnes St., Clayton-le-Moors.

Jones, Edward of Barnes St., Clayton-le-Moors. A married Man. He was carried out with a broken leg.

Keelan, Peter aged 13, of 43 Sparth Rd., Clayton-le-Moors. A drawer. He was slightly burnt and gave evidence at the inquest.

Leeming, Henry. A boy. (Age and other details are unknown).

Leeming, Moses of High St., Clayton-le-Moors.

Leeming, Thomas of Henry St., Clayton-le-Moors. A youth.

Metcalf, Lawrence of William St., Clayton-le-Moors. A getter. An elderly man he was known as '*Old Loll*'. He told the inquest that, "*I passed out at the time of the shake*". He had to crawl over the dead as he made his way out of the pit accompanied by Richard Shadlock. He was the uncle of Thomas Metcalf who was killed. He was also the father-in-law of Joseph Thornton who was killed.

Parker, Fred of 9 Crown St., Accrington.

Rawcliffe, George. Of Church.

Riding, Moses of 27 Henry St., Enfield.

Rushton, E. (No further details known).

Shadlock, John of Orange St., Accrington.

Shadlock, Richard. He gave evidence at the inquest, saying that he had been knocked over by the blast and had laid unconscious until the afternoon. He had then crawled for 200yds. over the dead and injured along a 27inch (685mm) high heading until he was found and brought out of the pit. Richard sustained internal injuries and also severe injuries to his chest and abdomen.

South, Henry. (The name William was also listed), of Malt St., Accrington. He claimed for his wife, Hannah, and four children. Mary Ann b.12-2-1874; Leonard b.16-3-1876; Riley b.2-6-1877 and Margaret Helen b.23-7-1878. There is a note in the Fund Register, which points out that there is only six weeks between Riley and Margaret Helen '*surely a mistake*'. Riley's date of birth had first been given as 2-6-1878. They also had another daughter Ann b.16-10-1871 who 'came of age' nine days after the disaster, and was unable to make a claim. '*2/6d to be stopped by resolution of Committee at this date Oct. 22/89*'. No reason is given. Henry spent some time in hospital at Buxton, Derbyshire in 1885. A Dr. Hartley sent in a bill for £1/17/0d (£1.85½p). He was also sent to London in February 1888 for treatment. The family came off the fund in July 1892.

Sutcliffe, George of 12 Bank St., Church. '*Injured by being gassed*'. He had a wife Betty and three children: Thomas Henry, b.4-9-1875; Mary b.16-7-1878 and George b.10-4-1884. There is a note in the Fund register, '*2/6d to be clipped by resolution 22 Oct. 89*' next to the names of George and Mary. No reason is given. At a later date the relief was reduced from 10/- (50p) to 5/- (25p) and then increased to 7/6d (37½p). Two more children were born after the explosion. '*At a meeting held on March 21ˢᵗ 1890 at the Town Hall, Accrington it was resolved to award 2/6d per week additional to a child born after explosion on Aug. 30ᵗʰ 1884, named Elizabeth Alice Rawcliffe until she attains 13 years of age*'. It would appear there was no allowance made for the other child.

Swales, William aged 15 of Victoria St., Church. A drawer who gave evidence at the inquest.

Taylor, Christopher Napoleon St., Clayton-le-Moors. A claim was made for two children: Charlotte b.28-3-1881, and Francis b.4-7-1882.

Threlfall, Lawrence of Altham. (No further details known).

Threlfall, Thomas, of Henry St., Church. (No further details known).

Walsh, John of 2 Birtwistle St., Accrington. He claimed for his wife Jane and a son William, b.4-9-1883.

Walsh, William aged 17,of Birtwistle St., Accrington. A drawer for William Warburton. He was a lodger with the Warburton family.

Walton, John of Henry St., Clayton-le-Moors; an address of High St., Clayton-le-Moors is also given. He claimed for his wife, Hannah, and two children: Elizabeth b.20-11-1883 and Nancy b.9-9-1884. They were then living at 267 Accrington Rd., Burnley. In March 1887, Mrs. Walton was living at 150 Cog Lane, Burnley, when she made a claim for support in her own right. She was awarded 5/- (25p) per week. John was sent to London for treatment in February 1888. From October to December 1888, John was in the workhouse and his sister, a Mrs. Hargreaves, claimed for the children. A Dr. Wilson billed the Fund in February 1889 for £2/13/4d (£2.67p). In Oct. 1889, Mrs. Walton's claim was disallowed. From March 1890, the pay book was signed by an Ann Walton? There is a notation in the Pay Book *'taken to the workhouse Feb. 5/91. I paid his brother Feb. 6 who said he had kept him'*. There was no further payment made until 16th September 1892, when a Nancy Stringer put in a claim for the children. She was awarded 10/- (50p) per week. This continued until Nancy Walton came of age in September 1891. John Walton died in the Whittingham Asylum on February 6th 1902.

Warburton, William. He was taken home injured along with his drawer William Walsh, who lodged with the family. His wife who was confined to bed awaiting the birth of a child had to give up her bed to accommodate the injured men.

Wolstenholme, John of Canal St., Clayton-le-Moors. A youth. (No further details known).

Wolstenholme, Robert Henry of Canal St., Clayton-le-Moors. (No further details known).

Yates, Edward. His nickname was *'Leather Patch'*. He had been brought out of the pit badly gassed. He suffered till 19th April 1886, when he fell over and died. His wife, Elizabeth made a claim for support. She was awarded 15/- (75p) per week. This was reduced to 5/- (25p) in Oct. 1889, then reduced again to 2/6d (12½p). No reason is given. This was stopped October 22nd 1890.

A scene at the pit mouth as depicted in 'The Graphic', 17-11-1883.

A number of medical bills were paid for out of the relief funds. These bills were not only for the injured, but were also for treating some of the relatives of those who were killed. A lady named Mary Mann, was allowed temporary relief of 10/- (50p) for four weeks from 8th January. 1892.

Two bills are recorded from a Dr. Bastion for treating Henry South and John Walton. One for £39/16/0d (£39.80p) for advice only, and the other for £1/1/8d (£1.07p) was for medicine. Both of these men suffered for years and never really recovered

Recorded in the Log books.

The schools in the area felt the immediate impact of the disaster. Some references to the explosion can be found in the school Log books.

Saint Mary's R. C. School Clayton-Le -Moors.
Nov. 9th 1883.

'An explosion took place in a colliery in this neighbourhood on Wednesday morning. Three of our boys were killed and three more seriously injured'.

Oakenshaw Wesleyan
Nov. 9th 1883.

'On Wednesday morning an explosion took place in the Moorfield pit belonging to the Altham Col. Co., by which nearly 70 persons lost their lives including'.

'James Atherton, Job Whittaker Haworth, killed. Ben Atherton, Henry Leeming, wounded at the same time'.

Nov. 16th

'Average & Fees still low, some of the children being at home to attend on the injured'.

St. James Mission, Clayton-Le-Moors.
Nov. 7th 1883.

'Very few children at school owing to an explosion at the coal pit'.

Nov. 9th

'Attendance still very small'.

Nov. 12th

'Attendance still small owing to the accident'.

County Borough of Bury.

Holt, Mayor.

CONDITIONS
UPON WHICH

CHILDREN are entitled to WORK
HALF-TIME and FULL-TIME.

HALF-TIME.

A Child of 12 YEARS OF AGE is entitled to a Certificate TO WORK HALF-TIME:

1,—If such child has attended 300 TIMES IN EACH YEAR in not more than 2 Schools for 5 years, whether consecutive or not,

OR

2.—If such child has passed the 3rd STANDARD (Labour Examination) and would IN THE OPINION OF THE COMMITTEE BE NECESSARILY AND BENEFICIALLY EMPLOYED.

FULL-TIME.

A child BETWEEN 13 AND 14 YEARS OF AGE is entitled to a Certificate TO WORK FULL-TIME:

1.—If such child has attended 350 TIMES IN EACH YEAR in not more than 2 Schools for 5 years, whether consecutive or not,

OR

2.—If such child has passed the 5th STANDARD (Labour Examination).

JOHN HASLAM,

Corporation Offices, Bank Street, Bury,
31st December, 1900.

Clerk to the School
Attendance Committee.

Charles Vickerman & Sons, Printers, Bookbinders, &c., 19, Union Square, Bury.

THE ALTHAM COLLIERY EXPLOSION RELIEF FUND

A meeting was convened by Alderman Lightfoot, the ex-Mayor of Accrington, in the Courtroom at Accrington Town Hall on the evening of the 12th of November 1883. There had been some attempt to form a committee prior to this meeting.

The fund was set underway with a subscription of 50 guineas from the Bishop of Manchester and an anonymous subscription of £100 from Glasgow. Further subscriptions had been made by Sir Ughtred Kay-Shuttleworth, £20; Mr. F.W. Grafton, £50; Alderman Lightfoot, 40 guineas; Mrs. Bunting, £5; Mr. Ellis Lever, Bolton, £20; Mr. Appleby, £100; Mr. Kerr for Steiner & Co. £100; Councillor Smith of Springhill, the new Mayor, 50 guineas; John Anderton and family £100; Messrs. Simpson & Co. £75; Lodge of Equality of Freemasons 10 guineas; East Lancashire Soap Co. £50 and Thos. Haworth & Son £100.

At the time of the meeting a sum amounting to over £3,000 had been raised. £100 was raised in street collections, £200 was raised in the Church collection. Other monies came from the private donations:- £500 from the Altham estates, £50 from Mr. Pickup, the owner of Rishton Colliery; £20 from Sir Joseph Peace MP; £20 from Lady Palmer of Southampton; and £25 from Mr. & Mrs Drew of Lowerhouse, Burnley.

A Letter from the Queen.

At a meeting of the Relief Committee at Accrington Town Hall on Tuesday evening, the following letter was read:- *'Windsor Castle, November 25th 1883. Sirs,- I have duly laid before the Queen your letter reporting the melancholy conditions of the widows and orphans of those who have lost their lives in the colliery accident at Altham. Her majesty was much grieved to read this account, and has commanded me to inform you that she will be glad to send a contribution of £50 to the relief fund.- I have the honour to be, sir, your obedient servant, HENRY F. PONSONBY.-To the Mayor of Accrington.'*

Among the contributions received was one from the Duke of Westminster of £20.

Letters to the Accrington Times.

Sir,- The terrible calamity which has so recently occurred in our midst again recalls our attention to the very many dangers to which our colliers are constantly exposed, not the least of which is that arising from the accumulation of foul and explosive gas. This is and always will be one of the most fertile sources of accident so long as the men are required to carry oil lamps about with them. The only sure and effectual cure for this evil is in the adoption of the incandescent system of electric lighting for our coalmines. A proper application of this beautiful system of lighting would not only render danger on this score nil, but would also provide a vastly superior light, contributing not only to safety but also to comfort. The little additional outlay, which its adoption would entail, is no reason why the colliery proprietors should not use it for the protection and benefit of the vast numbers of men in their employ.

I am, etc. George Wilkinson
Kenyon's Temperance Hotel, Accrington.

Sir,- I was very sorry indeed on Wednesday night to hear the church bells ringing and shouting with might and main, as if we had just received intelligence of something to universally rejoice at, whereas during the day we had received one of the greatest shocks Accrington has ever known (the Altham Colliery Explosion). Surely we have a spark of feeling left yet for those in such great trouble; but how must these bells ringing at such a time have sounded to those in such great anxiety and bereavement, and who had perhaps lost their whole? Why simply mockery. These bells would say there were people who could not weep with those who wept, even for a single day, and could not even for a single day put off their own cause for rejoicing, even in the face of such a great calamity. Shame, I say, on those who are responsible for this mockery. Trusting this will meet their eye, and apologising for troubling you,- I remain, yours faithfully, J.T.D.

The Central Committee:- Distribution.

The Central Relief Committee, which had been in existence since the week following the disaster, had their first full meeting on the 20th of November 1884. The committee consisted of:-

W. Smith, J.P., Mayor of Accrington, Chairman.
Swain Rhodes, J.P., Deputy Mayor, Vice Chairman.
Mr. R.H. Rowland, Treasurer.
Mr. John P. Hartley, Hon. Secretary.
Rev William Sharp, Altham
Mr. W. Hallam, Moorfield, near Colne
Mr. George Walmsley, J.P., Church
Mr. W.W. Simpson. J.P., Church
Mr. W.H. Marsden, Church
Mr. James Kerr, Church
Mr. John Clegg, Chairman of the Local Board, Church
Mr. W. Metcalf, Chairman of the Local Board, Oswaldtwistle
Mr. J. Tennant, Chairman of the Local Board, Clayton-le-Moors
Mr. A. Appleby, J.P., Clayton-le-Moors
Mr. Joshua Hacking, Clayton-le-Moors
Mr. Thomas Calvert, Clayton-le-Moors
Mr. Joseph Walker, Clayton-le-Moors
Mr. H.L. Wilson, Clayton-le-Moors
Mr. Jos. Haydock, Chairman of the Local Board, Great Harwood
Mr. Fletcher, Dunkenhalgh
Mr. James Lomax, J.P., D.L., Representative T. Wensley
Mr. Alderman Entwisle, J.P., Accrington
Mr. John Howard, Globe Works, Accrington

Mr. E.W. Horne, Accrington

Mr. William Bury, Accrington

Mr. John Anderton, Accrington

Mr. G.W. Macalpine, Accrington

Mr. Abraham Ashworth, Accrington

Mr. James Hanson, Chairman of the Local Board, Rishton

Mr. G.L. Campbell, Secretary to the Lancashire and Cheshire Miners' Permanent Relief Fund Society, Wigan

The fund had raised £13,667/19/0d, the vast majority of the money coming from public donation. In the twelve months prior to the meeting £1,868 0s 0d had been paid out to the relatives of the dead and injured £1,020/14/2d was for funeral expenses. Various other expenses had been incurred in the running of the fund, e.g. medical fees, printing and postage and solicitors' fees etc. A £10 gift was donated to the Padiham District Nurses Fund. Testimonials of £20 to local nurses and £25 to the Hon. Secretary for services rendered were also paid. A sum of 18 shillings was paid out for a suit of clothes, for whom is not stated. The bulk of the monies, £10,000, was invested with Accrington Corporation at 3.5%.

There were forty-eight adults in receipt of relief, three of these being men who had been injured in the explosion and were still unable to return to work. There were ninety-five children on the books, each of whom received 2/6d (12½p) per week in support. Since the explosion, four children had died, £5 was paid out of the fund towards the cost of burial. There were three children born and the family received £2 in addition to the 2/6d. Two children had already attained the age of 13 years and ceased to be classed as dependants.

One of the widows, Mrs. Brown, had remarried; as per resolution she received £25. Over the years many of the widows remarried, most of them within two years. Each received £25 from the fund although their children still remained on the books as dependants.

The Clayton-le-Moors Relief Committee.

Due to the large number of victims who resided in the Clayton area, a separate committee was formed to deal with their immediate needs. They worked under the auspices of the Central Committee based at the Town Hall, Accrington, who dealt with the rest of the families, irrespective of where they lived.

I have only been able to trace one set of recorded minutes for any committee meetings, those of the Clayton-le-Moors sub-committee. I have reproduced them here almost in their entirety. From this short record it is possible to glean some idea of the problems which were met within the days immediately following the catastrophe:-

At a meeting of the Clayton representatives, held at Accrington, after the General Public meeting in the Town Hall, it was resolved that Arthur Appleby J.P. be appointed Chairman of this Committee.

It was resolved that Joshua Hacking be appointed Secretary. It was also resolved to invite several other men to meet the representative of the Central Committee at the Mechanics' Institute, Clayton-le-Moors the following morning (Saturday) at 9-30.

The question of inviting the clergy to meet the representative was also discussed. It was decided that as they would be much engaged during the day with funerals, it would be better not to do so.

The committee held their first meeting at the Mechanics' Institute Clayton-le-Moors on Saturday 10th November. At the meeting the list of killed and injured was divided into seven districts. Each district was allocated to two visitors. The visitors set out immediately to assess the situation regarding the relatives of the victims. The meeting was adjourned until two o'clock in the afternoon

William Campbell, the Secretary of the Lancashire and Cheshire Permanent Miners' Relief Society, attended this meeting. He was later to become a member of the Central Committee. With the benefit of his experience in other disasters in the coalfields, he was able to give the committee some sound advice. This was to obtain particulars of all persons directly affected by the calamity i.e. the widows, wives, children, brothers and sisters of the killed and injured etc. This list to be compiled and submitted to the Central Committee the following Monday evening. The Chairman was instructed to advise Mr. Smith the Mayor of Accrington and Mr. Kerr of Church to this effect and ask them if they would get the information required from their districts.

It was resolved that the visitors who had worked throughout the day should be invited to join the committee, and that all the Clergy, Ministers of Religion and the preachers of the non-denominational chapels in the township should also be invited to join the committee.

When the full committee was finally constituted it consisted of:-

Mr. Arthur Appleby, J.P., Chairman.	Mr. Thomas Kenyon
Mr. Thomas Calvert, Vice Chairman.	Mr. Stephen Holgate
Mr. Joshua Hacking, Secretary	Mr. Mark Johnson
Mr. James Tennant	Rev. W. J. Lake
Mr. H. L. Wilson	Mr. R. E. Bray
Mr. Joseph Walker	Mr. T.K. Paython
Mr. Edmund Haywood	Mr. J. Hothersall
Mr. James Smith	Mr. Charles Williams
Mr. James Broadley	Mr. Willsdon
Mr. J. Ashworth	Mr. J. H. Hill
Mr. Francis Leary	

From the minutes.

The Chairman, Vice Chairman and four members of the Clayton Committee also sat on the Central Committee. The following are from the minutes:-

Monday 12th Nov. 1883.

At the meeting, Joshua Hacking resigned the Secretaryship and James Smith took over the job. It was resolved that nominees be appointed to start distributing aid in the form of money, blankets, sheets etc. A request was made to the Central Committee to secure the services of two extra lady nurses.

Friday 16th Nov. 1883.

Dr. Tattersall attended, to ask for the services of a barber to attend to the injured. Resolved to hire a barber at a fee of 1/- (5p) for each case. Resolved to pay the burial fees as the accounts were sent in.

Friday 23rd Nov. 1883.

Resolved that the Chairman suggest to the Central Committee the desirability of making some suitable acknowledgement for the kind and efficient manner the lady nurses have attended to the requirements of the sufferers. Resolved that the burial fees be reimbursed to the following families:

Family of late John Edge.	Paid to Mr. Hasilwood		£13/6d. (67$\frac{1}{2}$p)
Do	Thomas Edge	Do	12/6d (62$\frac{1}{2}$p)
Do	Osbaldeston (father), to James Home		15/0d. (75p)
Do	Osbaldeston (son)	Do	9/9d. (49p)

On a motion by Mr. Tennant it was resolved that in cases where there was any doubt of any person having been sick who may be applying for relief, that in all such cases a medical certificate must be produced before the application can be allowed.

On a motion of Mr. Wilson it was resolved that no order shall in future be given for groceries by anyone except the District Visitor, and in that case it must be out of funds already granted by the Committee.

Thursday 29th Nov. 1883.

The Chairman reported that all the injured cases were now taken over and their wants being attended to by the Miners' Insurance Fund and that no orders for food or materials must now be given by the Committee.

The Chairman reported that he had passed on the Committee's suggestion, made at their last meeting, '*that some suitable acknowledgement should be made to the two nurses*'. The Central Committee accepted the suggestion leaving this Committee to carry out the idea as they decided best. It was resolved that Messrs. Wilson, Calvert and Hacking be appointed as a sub-committee to draw up an address to each of the nurses and that they be empowered to get the same properly written and illuminated.

The Committee now awarded to each widow 5 shillings (25p) and to each child 2/6d (12$\frac{1}{2}$p) per head up to 13 years of age. This being the rate of allowance permanently fixed by the Central Committee.

Resolved that all persons entitled to receive an allowance, in future fetch the same from such person as may be duly authorised to pay the same.

Resolved that James Smith be appointed disburser pro-tem. and that attendance be given at the Local Board office on Friday evenings for such purposes from 6pm to 7pm.

The following persons having lent blankets to the sufferers. It was resolved that they be supplied with new ones in their place.

Mrs. Cronshaw, Napoleon St.

Mrs. W. Yates, 8 Clayton St.

Resolved that the following sums be awarded to the makers of soup towards their trouble and expenses-viz-

| Mrs. Elizabeth Procter | £2 |
| Miss Mary Edmundson | £1 |

Resolved that it be an instruction to get all bills in for next meeting.

The Chairman reported that the canvases made of the district for subscriptions by Messrs. James Sharples, Rothwell Hunt, George Riley and David Newsham amounted to the handsome sum of £143/9/10d. It was unanimously resolved *'that the best thanks of this Committee be tendered to the before-named gentlemen'*.

Thursday Dec. 20th

The Committee having considered the circumstances of the various families where single young men were killed with a view to assist the Central Committee in fixing the grant of money that should be made in each case. Case adjourned.

Friday 11th January 1884.

The Chairman reported that no decision had come to the Central Committee in considering the grants to be allowed where single young men had been killed.

It was resolved that the Secretary write to Mr. Macalpine to draw their Society, the Colliery Sick Club, together before the next Central Committee meeting to enable the Committee to make a special allowance in cases of death of single young men.

Resolved that blankets be allowed to Mrs. Paynton. Special allowances were made to the following persons:-

No. 9. Aaron Riding 5 shillings (25p) per week, so long as Colliery club pay.

No 17 James Scholes 10 Shillings (50p) per week for one month.

No 31 Wm. Taylor's widow 7/6 (35p) so long as incapacitated for work.

No 44 J. T. Hall 5 shillings (25p) per week for 3 months commencing January 12/84.

No 43 John Crabb £3 to be allowed to his mother for Mr. Bray.

Nos, 32/33 Mrs Almond 10/- (50p) per week from May 12/84.

Resolved that the sub-committee present the illuminated addresses to the nurses.

Resolved that Mr. Appleby see Mr. Smith about taking over the Secretaryship.

Thursday 20th March 1884.

Mr. Appleby submitted a tabulated statement of account of monies received and expended by him showing that he had handed over a balance of £13/16/8d to J. Smith, the Secretary. It was resolved that Messrs. Wilson and Holgate audit the accounts for Mr. Appleby's satisfaction. Mr. Appleby reported he had still about 20 sheets left. Resolved that *'they be given amongst widows so far as they will go'*.

In the matter of paying death claims in cases of single young men who were members and half-members of the Colliers' Club, the Committee resolved that all such claims should be paid in one sum.

Proposed by Mr. Ashworth and resolved the payment to the widows be made every two weeks.

Proposed by Mr. Hacking seconded by Mr. Walton and unanimously resolved that the best thanks of the Committee be given to Mr. Appleby for the painstaking and able manner in which he had conducted these meetings, the work of the Local Distributing Committee having now come to an end.

It would appear that at about this time the full committee was dissolved and that the welfare work would from now on be supervised by four of the principal members.

Monday 24th March 1884.

This meeting, the last one recorded in the minute book, was held in Mr. Appleby's office at the Local Board offices whereas all the other meetings had been held at the Mechanics' Institute. Four men attended, Messrs. Appleby, Wilson, Calvert and Hacking.

The Committee carefully awarded to each death claim the sum due to them, according to their membership of the Colliery Club.

In the matter of J. T. Hall's claim, case No. 44 on the list, it was proposed by Mr. Hacking, seconded by Mr. Calvert, and resolved that the Central Committee be recommended to place the case on the permanent list of 5 Shillings (25p) per week, and in the event of it not being granted that the allowance of £8 be made.

James Smith, the Secretary to the Clayton-le-Moors Local Board, was later appointed Almoner by the Central Committee, an appointment he still held in 1903.

James Macintosh was later offered the management of Moorfield and Whinney Hill collieries, which he declined. He never returned to the mines. He became the landlord of the Greyhound Hotel and also had some farming interests. James suffered for years from the effects of breathing in the afterdamp during the rescue operations and he was also prone to fits of deep depression. His wife died at Whitsuntide 1893 leaving behind six young children. On the tenth anniversary of the colliery disaster James Macintosh committed suicide, at the age of forty.

Miners from Moorfield and Whinney Hill collieries led the funeral cortege on the journey to Altham and the shops along the route remained closed as a mark of respect

For many years in the main room of the Greyhound Hotel at Altham West, there was a framed list of those who lost their lives in the disaster. In 1994 this list was removed to Altham parish church. Mr. Terry Woods a calligrapher from Oswaldtwistle created an illuminated scroll of the dead, which is now in the library at Clayton le Moors.

A plaque was affixed to stone-work of Pilkington's Bridge (Dickie Brig) to commemorate the 110th anniversary of the disaster in October 1993 by a former Hyndburn Mayor Councillor Mrs. Cathleen Thom.

Coal mining ceased at Whinney Hill in 1932. The shafts were left open to ventilate the workings at Moorfield. These were later filled in and capped off. A large housing estate has been built on the land once occupied by Whinney Hill Colliery, and the NORI brick works. The site of the shafts can be found to the right of the road going up to Whinney Hill from the traffic lights at the Greyhound Hotel. Directly above the entrance to the estate a small area has been fenced off and trees have been planted directly over the shafts.

In 1948, the year after the nationalisation of the coal industry, work in the Lower Mountain seam ceased. The following year the workings in the Upper Mountain seam were abandoned, bringing coal production at Moorfield to an end. The shaft has been capped off but not filled in.

The coking plant stayed in production until 1962 when it was forced to close due to heavy trade losses, 253 men losing their jobs. Apart from a few buildings, the site was cleared by the late 1960s. It is now an industrial trading estate.

Glossary of words and phrases appearing in the text, with other explanations.

Afterdamp. A mixture of gasses left over after a firedamp explosion, very low in oxygen and high in carbon monoxide. After an explosion in a coal mine, afterdamp would often claim more victims by suffocation than did the actual explosion.

Air Splitting. See Split Ventilation.

Assistant Fireman. An official below the rank of fireman; in later years they were known as Shotfirers.

Barometer. An instrument for measuring atmospheric pressure. Low or falling barometric readings often coincides with high gas emissions from the coal surrounding strata or old workings. A barometer was kept at every coal mine and it was the duty of the officials to take a reading at the beginning of their shift before descending into the mine. The coal industry now uses a Barograph, an automatic barometric instrument.

Blower. The sudden emission of firedamp (gas) from the coal seam or the surrounding rock. Blowers varied in strength from small emissions that made a hissing sound to the more violent that created a harsh screeching noise that could be heard at a great distance. Blowers would often continue for weeks.

Board or Bord. A roadway driven through the coal or rock to form a working district.

Board and Pillar. A method of working a coal seam by driving roadways, boards, through the solid coal and every few yards working off at right-angles to the left and right thereby leaving pillars of coal to support the roof of the mine. When the bords had reached their limits, a method of retreat working would begin and the pillars would be mined leaving the roof to collapse

Bottom Bed. A local name for the Lower Mountain seam.

Brattice. A wooden partition covered with brattice cloth used to divert and control the air supply. A brattice built along the centre of a roadway was known as a midfeather. Air would pass along one side of the brattice, ventilate the heading where the men were working and then return down the other side of the brattice.

Brattice Cloth. A heavy hessian material impregnated with a tarry preservative to seal the weave and make the cloth air-proof. Used to cover a wooden framework when constructing a brattice.

Brow, Brew. A steep inclined roadway in the mine. Above ground a brow is the top of a hill.

Cage. The lift in a mine shaft for raising and lowering men and materials. First introduced by John Curr of Sheffield in about 1787. The cage at Moorfield was a two-decker. The cage had one deck above the other; each deck would hold four tubs with an average $4^1/_2$ cwt. of coal in each tub. When 'man riding' (i.e. carrying men) the cage would carry 16 men, 8 to a deck.

Collier. From the Middle English, Colyer. The name collier was first applied to a charcoal burner long before it was associated with coal mining. In coal mining it was the name given to an experienced coal-getter working at the coalface. It later became synonymous with any man who worked underground in a coal mine.

Creep. The gradual lifting of the floor, or the gradual caving of the roof and sides in a flowing action. Caused by the weight of the surrounding strata.

Dataler. Originally a man who worked and was paid by the day. In later years the man would be in full-time employment. He would be paid a flat-rate wage as opposed to the colliers who were paid on a piece work system i.e. by the amount of coal they sent out of the pit.

Dip workings. When a coal seam was on a steep incline a level roadway would be driven across the seam. Coal that was worked to the low side of the level was known as the dip workings or the dip side. Coal being worked going up hill from the level was known as the rise side.

District. The underground workings in a coal mine would be sectioned off into districts. Each district would be under the charge of a particular fireman or deputy who first and foremost would be in charge of the smooth running of the district and keeping up the production of coal. After nationalisation his first responsibility would be for the safety of the men.

Door boy or **Door-tenters**. The youngest of the boys employed in the mines. His job was to open and close the ventilation doors to allow the drawer to push his tub through without having to stop. Before 1842, children as young as eight years old, both boys and girls, would be employed as door tenters.

Doors, Ventilation. Wooden, or in some cases metal, doors which were used to close off a short roadway which ran between the roadway along which the clean air came into the mine and the roadway along which the foul air went out of the mine. The doors allowed the men and tubs to travel from one road to the other and prevented the clean air coming into the workings from the foul air that was being drawn out of the workings by the ventilation system.

Door Tenter. Another name for the door boy. See **Door boy**.

Downcast Shaft. The shaft down which clean air was drawn into the mine.

Drawer. Boys and young men employed to bring empty tubs to the collier and take away the full ones. Depending on conditions, this could be the hardest work in the mine.

Drawing. The work of the drawer. The action of pushing the tubs along the rails.

Engine Plane or **Engine Level**. A roadway in the mine along which the tubs were transported using a chain rope haulage.

Fault. A fracture in the rock strata which often displaces a seam of coal. A fault also creates cracks in the rock above and below a coal seam, in which the firedamp escaping from the coal accumulates.

Firedamp. See **Gas**.

Fireman. The man in charge of a working district in a mine. He would inspect the district and make sure the ventilation was keeping the district clear of gas. In the early years, he would also be responsible for the production and movement of coal. In some areas the fireman was known as a deputy.

Fizzing. The sound created by gas escaping from the strata. In extreme cases it was said to scream and roar like a steam train.

Furnace Ventilation. A method of ventilating a mine by having a large furnace at the base of the upcast shaft. The hot air rising up the shaft drew the foul air out of the mine to be replaced by clean air being drawn down the downcast shaft.

Gas. Methane, CH_4 Carburetted Hydrogen or marsh gas, known in coal mines as firedamp formed by the decomposition of organic matter. It is a colourless, tasteless and odourless gas, which when mixed at about 15% to air becomes highly explosive. A massive influx of gas from a cavity in the coalseam filled with firedamp under high pressure would, when it was broached, escape with such force that it could cause an explosion.

Getter. A local name for a collier, the man who worked at the coalface, mining (i.e. getting) the coal with pick and shovel.

'Getting without light'. To put out your lamp by accident was to *'get without light'*. A common occurrence when oil lamps were in use.

Gig Road. See **Jig road**.

Half-timer or **Short-timer**. A child on reaching the age of twelve who was able read and write would then be allowed to work as a half timer. The child would be able to spend half their time in education and a similar period of time at work. Those who were unable to gain their school certificate would have to remain at school until coming of age at thirteen.

Heading. A roadway driven into the coal. Individual getters would work off each side of the heading to create a working place known as a stall. A much larger roadway driven through rock was known as a hard heading.

Head Fireman. An official below the under-manager at a colliery, equivalent to the modern day Overman.

Head Gear. The winding gear (wheels) and supporting structure at the top of the shaft.

Hooker-on. The man who loaded the cage at the bottom of the shaft. He also signalled the winding engineman when to raise the cage.

Inbye. Into the mine away from the shaft, the opposite of outbye. To travel inbye was to go into the workings.

Inspector of Mines. An official appointed under the Coal Mining Act to inspect a mine at any given time to ascertain that the requirements of the Act were being carried out. He also investigates serious or fatal accidents.

Jig road or **Gig road**, also known as a **Jinney Road**. A roadway on which a self-acting haulage system was in use. A large wheel with a steel rope passing around it was situated at the top of the steep inclined roadway. Full tubs travelling down hill would be attached to one end of the rope. The weight of the tubs would be used to pull the empties up the incline. The speed of the tubs would be controlled by a hand brake attached to the wheel.

Jig Tenter or **Jinney Tenter**. The man who controlled the speed of the tubs going up and down the jig road. .

Landing Plates. Cast iron or steel plates surrounding the area where the tubs were unloaded from the cage. The plates would become highly polished and very slippery. It took some skill to manoeuvre the tubs especially if the plates were wet. The force of the explosion coming up the shaft lifted the landing plates at Moorfield.

Level. A roadway through the coal, off which the headings would be driven to form a working district.

Lower Mountain Mine. The lower of the two seams worked at Moorfield, also known as the 'bottom bed'. The other seam was the Upper Mountain Mine.

Man riding. When men were riding up or down the shaft in the cage.

Main Level. The main level along which the tubs were transported to and from the top of the jig road.

Methane. See **Gas**.

Mid-feather. See **Brattice**.

Mine. A local name for a coal seam, indigenous to Lancashire.

Mountain mines. The two coal seams, known as the mountain mines, were first extensively worked in the hills above the valley that runs from Rawtenstall to Bacup, the Rossendale Valley. This is why they were named the mountain mines.

Of age. A child reaching the age of thirteen was said to be 'of age' and was allowed to leave school to take up full time employment. See also **Half timer**.

Onsetter. The man at the base of the shaft who signalled to the winding engine man when it was safe to wind the cage up the shaft. His counterpart at the top of the shaft on the surface was called the banksman.

Pillar and stall, **Straight and pillar** and **Bord and pillar**. All methods of extraction especially in the Northwest, where pillars were left in to support the roof, compared with longwall working, where all the coal is extracted. Later, in pillar and stall, the pillars were also extracted, leaving the roof to collapse.

Pipers. Gas which came out of the coal. In the Durham coalfield the miners would drive a thin copper pipe into the hole and set fire to the gas. These gas-lights were used to illuminate the main roadways. Many of them continued to burn for many years.

Pit Bank. The area surrounding the top of the shaft.

Points. A point on the tub rails where the tubs could be shunted from one track to another.

Quarter (measure). From the Latin quartarius, one fourth part. The quarter was a measure of capacity which has been in use since the 13th century. The quarter varied depending on what goods were being measured. In 1602, coal was sold at 6d. (2$^{1}/_{2}$p) a quarter. (Lancs). In 1820, in Devonshire, a quarter of Welsh coals or culm equalled 16 heaped 'bushels'.

Return Airway. The roadway along which the foul air travelled on its way out of the mine.

Rig. A localised name for a fault. See **Fault**.

Rise side. Workings going 'to the rise' or rise side away from the main level, are going up the inclination or slope of the seam. Those going 'to the dip' are going in the opposite direction.

Rope Haulage. See. **Self-acting**.

Scale. A current of air which ventilated the workings. The amount of gas emanating from the blower was so dense that it was able to stop the flow of air going along the roadways.

Self-acting incline. An inclined roadway down which coal was transported by means of a rope travelling around a pulley or a drum at the top of the incline. The weight of the loaded tub was sufficient to draw up the empty tubs attached to the other end of the rope on a second parallel track.

Sheet. Sheets of brattice cloth set up as a temporary measure to control the flow of air.

Short timer. See **Half-timer**.

Shotfirer. The man who fired the explosives in the mine. In later years he was known as a deputy.

Signalled Off. When the onsetter at the base of the shaft made the signal to the engine man to raise the cage, he was said to have '*signalled off*'.

Sledge or **Tram**. An oblong shaped board fitted with four wheels, used by the men to travel to and from their working places along the low roadway. A man would kneel on the board with one leg and use the other leg to propel the sledge along. They were also known as sleddes.

Splitting. See **Split Ventilation**.

Split Ventilation. The underground mine workings were sub-divided into separate ventilating districts. Each district would have its own supply of air uncontaminated with the foul air from the other districts. The main intake air was split into the different districts of the mine. All the foul air from the individual districts would eventually leave the mine via the main return air road and the upcast shaft.

Stoppings. A solid wall built from timber, stone, or brick across a roadway or entrance to old workings. They were built to restrict access of clean air into the old workings.

Sump hole. A large hole below the base of the shaft that was constructed to collect all the water coming out of the workings. The water would be then pumped out of the mine.

Top Bed. A local name for the Upper Mountain Mine (coal seam).

Tram. See **Sledge**.

Tub. A small four wheeled rail-tracked vehicle for carrying coal. Much like a large wooden box on wheels. The tubs at Moorfield had a capacity of $4^1/_2$ cwt. (228kilos).

Upcast Shaft. The shaft by which the used and foul air leaves the pit.

Upper Mountain Mine. The upper of the two seams worked at Moorfield, also known locally as the 'Top Bed.' The lower of the two seams was the Lower Mountain Mine or 'Bottom bed.'

Warnings. A warning written with chalk on a piece of timber or the blade of a shovel warning the men not to advance beyond that point. A verbal warning would be shouted when a shot was about to be fired.

'Welly Bottled'. To be full of beer, to have had a good drink, but not be drunk.

In Memoriam

Lines suggested on reading a report of the painful colliery explosion at Moorfield Colliery, near Accrington, November 7th, whereby upwards of sixty poor colliers lost their lives

"From the blossom of health to the paleness of death
It seems like the wink of an eye, or a breath."

OH! check not the tear that would start to the eye,
When you feel the full weight of a loving good-bye;
Have you lost some lov'd one? if so, you can tell
The full weight of grief in a final farewell.

Fron Accrington cries of deep anguish doth rise,
A gloom of despondency darkens the skies;
They mourn over lov'd ones in utter despair,
And grieve as they look on some dear vacant chair.

"Oh, could I have seen my dear lad e'er he died,
I might have sustained him", a poor mother cried;
"I almost imagine, at times, I can see,
My poor boy so patiently looking for me."

When they travers'd death's dark valley - let this thought cheer,
Though earth's friends were absent, a Divine Friend was near;
'Tis well you should sorrow and moan o'er your loss -
In your sorrow remember the thief on the cross:

When no earthly friend was able to save,
He cried for forgiveness, and Jesus foregave.
The prayer of our heart is that souls were set free,
In reply to the prayer "Lord, remember Thou me".

Let us look at the sorrowful picture again,
And forget not the mourners whilst we think of the men.
Gallant fellows are those who risk their own lives,
To sustain through their labours their children and wives.

May the blessing of God rest on those who are left,
On the widows and orphans of guardians bereft;
Whilst the forms of the bread-winners rest 'neath the sod,
We would leave their dear souls to a merciful God.

"Be you also ready!" - How solemn the text!
Yet how true; and we know not whose turn may be next;
Our comrades, so suddenly taken away,
Were cheerful and merry a week since to-day.

Oh that men would but turn from the pathway of sin,
What joy and contentment and peace would it bring;
If we throughout life on our God would rely,
We could show in the end how a Christian could die.

Those brave-hearted heroes we love and admire,
Who gallantly rescued their mates from the fire,
May the blessing of heaven rest on each volunteer,
Who offer'd assistance when danger was near.

With Christ in our heart we can stand every blast,
And smile when our years of probation are past;
If our hearts are kept pure, and Christ be our theme,
We shall meet with our loved ones, just over the stream.

Composed by The Miners' Friend

Subscribers

"Curry Alan", Laneside Avenue, Accrington
Doreen Ainscough, Oldham
Ms D. Ashburn Canham, Blackburn
Derek Aspin, Rochester, NY
Mrs. Edith Ayre, Ipswich
Eric Baines, Great Harwood
Gerald Baker, Bamford Crescent, Baxenden
M. V. Barcroft, Rawtenstall
Sheila Barker, Alston
Alan Birtwistle, St. Ives
Mrs C. D. Blowers, Ashford
Doreen Bowkley, Blackburn
Gary Brain, Oldham
Frank Bridges, Great Harwood
Neville & Barbara Bridge, Mellor
John D, Brown, Saddleworth
Steven J. Broadley, Burnley
Christine Bryant, nee Barrett, Rawtenstall
C. M. Campbell-Algar, Canterbury
H. C. Carr, Burnley Road, Huncoat
Nefyn Cardwell, Kidwelly
Mrs. R. Charnley, Whalley Road, Clayton
R. Cidzyn, Lancaster
Anne Coates, Craven Arms
J. Cook, Canada
May Cornwell, nee Johnson, Great Harwood
Clifford P. Cronshaw, Stockport
A. & S. M. Crook, Whalley Road, Clayton
K. S. & G. P. Crook, Northwich
Paul Crook, London
Robert Cunliffe, Wensley Avenue, Accrington
Derek Dalton, Parbold

Ian S. Dixon, Sparth Road, Clayton
Eddie Dodds, Fielding Lane, Oswaldtwistle
Bob & Wendy Dower, nee Wilson, Prestatyn
George Dyson, Bristol
Joan Edge, Castle Bromwich
Tim Entwistle, Great Harwood
Peter Franklin, Fountain Street, Accrington
Geoff Garnett, Stanhill Hall (2 copies)
Steve Garside, Huddersfield
Vincent Gee, Walkden
Edna Gorton, Worsley Court, Oswaldtwistle
John Gorton, Colchester
Eric Gowans, Preston
Josie R. Green, Royds Avenue, Accrington
Pauline A. Grimshaw, Kearsley
Gordon Hall, Earl Street, Clayton
Tom Halsall, Poynton
Gill Hamilton, Southport
Ken Hamlett, Middleton
Ken Hardacre, Great Harwood
L. A. Hardy
Thomas Hargreaves, Calgary
Peter Hart, Skipton
Gordon Hartley, Burnley
Eric Haworth, Northwich
Lawrence Haworth, Woking
Roy Hilton, Wymeswold
Dr. M. Hocking, Bristol
Barbara & Brian Hodgkinson, Ramsbottom
T. Houghton, Whalley
John M. T. Howat, Rawtenstall
T. A. Hunt, Colne
Rod J. Ireland, Leyland

Mr & Mrs B. M. Jackson, Penwortham
C. Jordan, Mallard Place, Oswaldtwistle
George Johnson, Foulridge
B. Kay, Clitheroe
Mrs. C. Kydd, Norwich (2 copies)
Christine Lamb, Mount Pleasant Street, Oswadltwistle
Brian Lead, Blackburn
Eric Lord, Lynwood Road, Huncoat
C. Loxham, Penwortham
John Lynch, Frederick Street, Oswaldtwistle
John Mannion, Limefield Street, Accrington
David W. Marshall, Simonstone
Catherine Martin, Ilford
Mr & Mrs A. J. Mason, Grange
Alan Henry Mullineaux, Plumstead
Mrs M. Noonan, Glenmore Close, Baxenden
Tony Norris, Burnley
Ralph Nuttall, Belfast
Mr B. & Mrs M. O'Rourke, Whalley Road, Clayton
Gcoff Oldham, Southwell ⸱
Ian Ormerod, Solihull
Harold Owen, Paddock Street, Oswaldtwistle (2 copies)
Richard Partington, Bolton
Roy Pearson, Boston
Doreen Pollard, nee Cross, Great Harwood
John Preston, Lowestoft
Bernard Rafferty, St. Helens
J. B. Reader, Lea
Colin V. Redmayne, Kings Road, Accrington
Michael R. Reid, Woking
Mary Riley, Whalley Road, Clayton
Colin Saxton, Stockport
Sheila Shaw, Mellor
John Shuttleworth, Oxford
Albert Smith, Pickup Bank
Chris & Linda Smith, Penwortham
Wendy Smith, nee Leeson, Haslingden Old Road, Oswaldtwistle
E. Stebbing, Crosby
A. Stigwood, Oldham
B. Sudell, Newchurch-in-Pendle (2 copies)
R. & M. Tattersall, Bacup
Geoff Taylor, Burnley Road, Accrington (2 copies)
Jeff Taylor, Great Harwood
D. Thomas, Windsor Avenue, Church
David R. Thornton, Lower Friar Hill Farm, Green Haworth (3 copies)
Anne Topping, Ashton-in-Makerfield
R. A. & H. Vaughan, Moss Hall Road, Accrington
Derek Ward, Blackburn
Jim Ward, Whitaker Street, Accrington
Mr. L. Warren, Manchester Road, Accrington
Dave Whalley, Guide
Jeff Whatmore, Merlin Drive, Oswaldtwistle
George White, Radcliffe
Agnes Whittam, Great Harwood
Wilky Wilkinson, Guildford
John E. R. Wrennall, Chorley
Annie Wright, Pickering